MYSTICISM AND MORALITY

[·]·[·]
[·]·[·]

MYSTICISM
AND MORALITY:
Oriental Thought and
Moral Philosophy

[·]·[·]

ARTHUR C. DANTO

[·]·[·]

COLUMBIA UNIVERSITY PRESS

NEW YORK

Columbia University Press   Morningside Edition

Columbia University Press   1987
New York

Library of Congress Cataloging-in-Publication Data

Danto, Arthur Coleman, 1924–
Mysticism and morality.

Reprint. Originally published: New York : Basic
Books, 1972.
Bibliography: p.
Includes index.
1. Ethics, Oriental.   2. Philosophy, Oriental.
I. Title.
[BJ962.D36 1987]   181   87-18242
ISBN 0-231-06639-2 (pbk.)

[·]

The Morningside Edition is

For A I N S L I E *and* S U E E M B R E E

[·]

Passage O soul to India!
Eclaircise the myths Asiatic, the primitive fables.

—WALT WHITMAN

A world of Dew
Is a world of dew and yet,
And yet . . .

—ISSA

PREFACE TO THE

MORNINGSIDE EDITION

In the concluding pages of his *Enquiry Concerning the Principles of Morals*, the skeptic and ironist David Hume laid before his enlightened readers a catalogue of practices that were deemed virtues in a darker era than his own: "Celibacy, fasting, penance, mortification, self-denial, humility, silence, solitude, and the whole train of monkish virtues." In the body of his text, Hume had advanced *usefulness* as the chief criterion against which questions of moral goodness were to be tested, for it seemed to him patent that "Whatever is valuable in any kind, so naturally classes itself under the division of the *useful* or the *agreeable* that it is not easy to imagine why we should ever seek further or consider the question as a matter of nice research or inquiry." It seemed no less patent to his incredulous spirit that the monkish virtues hopelessly fail this easy test. "They serve no manner of purpose," Hume confidently wrote, and they will accordingly be "everywhere rejected by men of sense." Hume went even further: so contrary did he judge those practices to be to our "natural unprejudiced reason, without the delusive glosses of superstition and false religion" that men and women of robust good sense will class them rather as *vices* than virtues—all the more so in that those who found it agreeable to pass their leisure hours in whist, flirtation, and amiable conversation would have scant inclination to indulge in sacerdotal austerities.

There can seldom have been an opportunity, in the salons and drawing rooms that were Hume's habitat when he was not engaged upon scholarly or diplomatic business, for a direct and confrontational dialogue between him and an active practitioner of monastic discipline. But were such an occasion ever to have arisen, it would soon have become plain that the issue between the philosopher and the anchorite would not have been a *moral* disagreement, not even one concerning the *principles* of morals. These the monk might agree with Hume had to do with what is useful to oneself or to mankind in large. The difference, rather, would finally be over matters of factual truth: what Hume dismissed as superstition and false religion, the monk would insist is true religion and rational belief. They differ only secondarily over how we ought to behave, and primarily over how the world really is.

Often, and even typically, what presents itself as a pitched controversy over moral practices disguises a basic disagreement over factual truth. Now Hume once advanced a celebrated thesis, debated to this day among philosophers, that there can be no logical connection between moral attitude and factual belief. We cannot validly deduce from a set of indicative premises a conclusion of an imperative form, saying what *ought* to be the case. There is accordingly a logically insuperable gap between "is" and "ought to be." The fact nevertheless remains that whatever may be the case in matters of formal deduction, we lose a set of reasons for behaving as we do when it turns out that what we had believed about the world begins to seem no longer true. If Christian belief were true, that there is an afterlife in which we are punished for misdeeds in this life, and that through the office of intercessive prayer we can modulate the harshness and duration of such punishments in our own case and even in the case of others, nothing could be more useful than self-abasement, the telling of beads, the recitation of orisons by specialists in convents and monasteries for the overall service of our soiled species.

There may be ultimate moral disagreements, disagreements which remain when there is no dispute concerning any matter of fact between the antagonists. But this would hardly have been the case between David Hume and his religious opponents. What we can say is that were the monk to be persuaded that his beliefs were indeed "delusive glosses of superstition and false religion" it would be difficult to imagine him persisting in practices of the sort Hume so sniffily condemns. He *could* continue to observe silence or to fast. But either he would have to find new grounds for these, which in any case will have lost their imperative character, or concede they have no basis in reason or revelation. And it is reasonable to expect that under an alternative view of the world, the practices would wither, as they had done in the precincts of Edinburgh or Paris in which Hume felt at all comfortable, intellectually or socially. Whatever philosophical distance may separate our moral views from our factual beliefs, they together make up the forms of life men and women actually live. As a matter of philosophical analysis, moral beliefs may be neither true nor false. They nevertheless fit together with beliefs that are either true or false to constitute together with them a form of life sufficiently organic that we must expect moral beliefs and moral practices to change when factual beliefs are altered or given up.

There is a further consideration. We cannot take over the moral beliefs of a form of life other than our own without also adopting the views of the world against which they alone make sense. The moral beliefs of the mystic can be acquired only at the cost of also accepting the mystic's vision of the real.

This view of the relationship between metaphysics and morality, or less portentously between moral attitude and factual belief, is of course invariant to any difference between East and West. When *Mysticism and Morality* appeared in 1973, the criticism was sometimes raised that I had overlooked the application of my analysis of Oriental systems of life to Western ways of life. It would never have occurred to me that there was not an absolutely parallel application, for the overall thesis of the book was tendered as a piece of moral philosophy concerning the objectivity of moral beliefs whatever their cultural locus. Nor was I supposing that the kind of cultural criticism in which I was engaged uniquely referred to the Oriental systems of thought that made up the subject of the book. If my analysis has the status of a weapon, it is one that could as easily have been used by adepts of an Oriental form of life against our own.

But this sounds altogether too adversarial. My philosophical aim, to be sure, was to show that the moral codes supported by the religions of the East could not be taken over as readily as yogic calisthenics or the eating of sushi, which have fit so smoothly into our cosmopolitan forms of life, just as blue jeans and rock music have fitted smoothly into otherwise exotic ways of thought and life. But the real aim of the book was to engage philosophically with systems of belief I greatly admired, and which I regretted I could not live. It had rarely happened that a philosopher of analytical persuasion had grappled with Oriental philosophy, which had been left as the province either of enthusiasts or scholars, and it is a matter of the greatest joy to me that a book in which I took such extreme pleasure—and which I had hoped would yield pleasure as well as information to others—returned to print. What the book offers is exactly the sort of debate that never, alas, took place between Hume and some opposing religious spokesman. Hume was altogether too scornful, and was himself too heavily criticized for his skepticism by the religious establishment of his time, for there ever to have really been what optimists call "dialogue" today. The figures in his *Dialogues Concerning Natural Religion* are finally too like-minded for their differences to resemble real and impassioned differences. Nor was Hume at all sanguine about the possibilities of serious discussion with zealots or fanatics. "Disputes with men pertinaciously obstinate in their principles are of all others the most irksome," he wrote as the first sentence in the *Enquiry Concerning the Principles of Morals.* Since my book appeared, waves of fundamentalism have inundated the world, and strife between alien forms of life has become bitter and unforgiving. The mere willingness to address moral differences across cultural barriers in the disinterested spirit of philosophical analysis already presupposes, as Hume evidently felt, an openness it is unreasonable to expect. But for just that reason the issues and the style of addressing them may have become more urgent than they could have been when I thought myself to be addressing a somewhat innocent counterculture. In any event the issues are too dangerous now just to leave to enthusiasts while too humanly important to leave as matters of mere scholarly investigation.

This is the third of my books to have been given a second life under the Morningside imprint of Columbia University Press. I am grateful beyond adequate expression to John Moore, the director of the Press, for this boon, and on the present occasion I am grateful as well to Abigail Meisel and Louise Waller for their sympathy, interest, and resoluteness in bringing back, for further use and disputation, a book for which I have great affection and in whose spirit I still have great confidence.

New York, 1987   A.C.D.

PREFACE

These are times when the moral fabric of our lives appears so rent that one must look with sympathy upon anyone who in desperation turns to other civilizations for guidance. The East has always held the promise of a deeply alternative existence, satisfying and pacific and exalting. It is hardly matter for wonder that its constant appeal is felt with an augmented intensity today. It is nevertheless an aim of this book to discourage the hope that a way through our moral perplexities may be found in the Orient. To be sure, much the same conclusion might be reached merely through keeping up with current events in Asia: *ad hominem* argumentation has a peculiar validity in matters of moral conduct. My reason, however, is more theoretical and abstract. It is that we cannot take over the moral beliefs of the East without accepting a certain number of factual beliefs—beliefs about the world—that such a system of moral beliefs presupposes. But the relevant factual beliefs cannot easily be assimilated to the system of beliefs that define the world for us. The fantastic architectures of Oriental thought, which it is also an aim of this book to sketch philosophically, are open to our study and certainly our admiration, but they are not for us to inhabit.

One does not passage casually to India, and it is partly to

provide a logical charm against our being distracted by a fantasy of Oriental salvation that I have written what may seem an anomalous book for an analytic philosopher to have done. But one may regard the book as an elaborate illustration of a thesis regarding the connection between facts and values— or between factual and valuational beliefs, since it is in the light of those factual beliefs that give them point and application that I discuss the *moral* beliefs of the Orient. I suspect the interest of the reader will lie, as in candor mine does as well, more with the illustration of the thesis than the theory that informs it. And the book may, apart from a somewhat austere vestibule, be appreciated as an essay on Oriental thought by readers largely indifferent to the remote preoccupations of meta-ethical inquiry. Yet, I write as a philosopher, rather than an Orientalist, and, hence, as one upon whom lies an obligation to chart, if not to span, the kinds of gaps that the one between fact and value is supposed to exemplify. My way across that gap is also the armature that defines from within the surface curvatures of my exposition and argument. And though the surface is exotic, since the thoughts depicted are alien and fabulous, it is the structure that justifies my meddling in such heady matters—*un barbare en Asie*, to borrow the wry title of Henri Michaux's somewhat analogous but marvelous book. So a few para-technical words are perhaps in order, lest structure succumb to surface, after the manner of an Indian temple.

In recent times, controversy in ethical theory has centered upon one main question and two distinct gaps. The question is how moral language is connected to the language we employ to describe the world; and the gaps are those that first divide moral terms from straightforwardly descriptive terms and then divide moral propositions from the morally neutral propositions that are intended to describe the world. The nature of these gaps varies more or less in accordance with the strategies for closing them, and the strategies themselves are responses to what their authors regard as a philosophically satisfactory answer to the question. Suppose, for example, one believes that the first gap is to be crossed by means of a definition, say a definition in some morally neutral vocabulary of the morally charged term "good"; and that the second gap is to be crossed by means of deducing a moral proposition from some set, however amplified, of morally neutral propositions. Now there are well-known arguments in philosophy, especially those of G. E. Moore and David Hume, according to which "good" cannot be defined in what Moore called "natural" terms, nor a proposition saying how we *ought* to act (or be) derived from premises that state only how we are or how the world is. One consequence of accepting these arguments is that moral concepts and moral maxims appear to be radically independent of factual ones, untethered by rules of meaning or ties of logic to the wider body of our concepts and beliefs and to our general understanding and representation of the world.

This has been appreciated in two ways. Either moral concepts answer to an adjunct kind of reality and designate specifically moral entities or qualities, which enjoy an existence absolutely independent of qualities and entities of other sorts, or they do not answer to reality at all, it being the office of moral language not to describe the world but to play some other role in human discourse: to *express* attitudes, to *enjoin* actions, to *commend* things, or whatever. There is no adjunct reality and no adjunct faculty, as Moore believed there was, for intuiting its presence. Instead there is a use of language adjunct to that we employ to describe the world, and this explains why we cannot assimilate moral idioms to morally neutral ones. Thus, with moral propositions questions of truth or falsity cannot begin to arise, and hence they cannot fit as conclusions in deductive arguments whose criteria of assessment presuppose the applicability of truth-values to premises and conclusions. Moral reasoning, then, is not capable of being represented in valid arguments, and moral propositions do not express knowledge. Both these approaches I believe wrong.

I cannot attempt here to catch the reader up in the cat's cradle of arguments that snare the student of ethical theory in a round of moves from Cognitivism to Non-Cognitivism or from Naturalism to Intuitionism, to give the main positions their textbook labels. Yet, one feels each position holds an authentic fragment of the truth. Naturalism is surely correct in holding that our moral concepts are not completely independent of our factual beliefs; Intuitionism is surely correct in insisting that the connections, whatever they may be, are not going to prove to be the philosophically favored ones of explicit definition and logical derivation; Non-cognitivism is surely correct in claiming that there is some residuum of meaning remaining when we subtract whatever is descriptive in moral terms and that this does not describe some further, recondite fact. The question then is what weaker connection than those exemplified by definition and entailment are available for binding moral language to that which by common consent does serve the purpose of recording the facts as we see them.

Briefly, my view is that without pretending to analyze moral terms or propositions into morally neutral discourse, moral terms apply to things and actions only on condition that descriptive ones do as well, and that moral propositions presuppose factual ones. And in especially the latter case, if these presuppositions are false, the moral ones are inapplicable whether it is appropriate to speak of them also as false or not. And this perhaps is as much of a connection as we require, at least for certain purposes, between factual and valuative discourse.

At least it is all that I require for purposes of the present essay. The civilizations of the East are defined through sets of factual and moral propositions pragmatically connected in the minds of their members since it is with reference to certain factual beliefs that those members would judge and act as moralists. The factual beliefs they take for granted are, I believe, too alien to our representation of the world to be grafted onto it, and in consequence their moral systems are unavailable to us. I say "our" representation of the world, though of course I imply no deep relativity of realities by this, since any beliefs we have are ones that the logic of belief requires us to hold as true. So our reality must be regarded by us as reality *tout court*. We can appreciate and understand, of course, forms of thought that it is closed to us to live. Thus, I hope, by fulfilling one aim of this book, which is to describe certain ways of reading the world, to be able to fulfill the other, which is to show that we cannot live a form of life that presupposes that reading. No one can save us but ourselves.

Paris and New York   A. C. D.

ACKNOWLEDGMENTS

In the conciliatory period of the late 1940s, the Japanese Government sent an exhibition of art to America which was to have an impressive effect upon American painting in the decade that followed. In my own case, I recall the almost cleansing impact of those clear forms and pure designs and light, unlabored atmospheres. I also recall the almost visceral revulsion I felt for the canvases of the High Venetian period I walked past upon leaving the Japanese show: they seemed indecently *fat*. This was a translation into aesthetic terms of a conflict in perspectives which motivates the present book. In any event, my interest in the Orient dates from then. It was an interest I was able to cultivate, however, primarily through a fortunate invitation to participate in the Oriental Humanities colloquium in Columbia College. For this I owe a special debt of gratitude to Professor William Theodore de Bary, now Vice President and Provost of Columbia University. For some years we sat at opposite ends of a seminar table and explored together the sometimes labyrinthine classics of the East.

I am grateful as well to the company of Oriental scholars I met through participation in that program, which constituted for me a special collective tutorial in Eastern thought. I want especially to mention Donald Keene, Ivan Morris, Marleigh

Ryan, Herschel Webb, Hans Bielenstein, Mason Gentzler, C. T. Hsia, John Meskill, Phillip Yampolsky, Chiang Yee, Burton Watson, Maan Madina, Eliot Deutsch, Ainslie Embree, Y. Hakeda, Barbara Miller, Robert Olson, Alex Wayman, Royal Weiler, and Andrew Yarrow.

A.C.D.

CONTENTS

MYSTICISM AND MORALITY

FACTUAL BELIEFS

AND MORAL RULES

We all make some distinction, however rough, between the factual and the moral beliefs of a community, and between factual and moral beliefs as such. There no doubt are many similarities between these two classes of belief, and although the distinction is difficult to define, it remains one that we all spontaneously make. And one criterion, which is often invoked when the question of marking the distinction is raised, is semantical: factual beliefs are either true or false, while moral beliefs are neither.

The semantical criterion would be obvious if moral and factual beliefs were expressed by sentences that were different in form, e.g., if factual propositions always were in the indicative mood and moral propositions always in the imperative. Everyone can see that "The window is shut" has to be either true or false, and that it is made so by the state of the window referred to by the sentence. But "Shut the window!" cannot sensibly be supposed true or false, because it states no fact but issues an order. To be sure, it may be said to *presuppose* a factual proposition in that the order cannot be carried out if the window is already shut: none of us can obey the command to stop running if we already have stopped running—though this would be a curious instance of insubordination indeed. In fact, it could not be insubordination at all. We cannot either obey or disobey a command based on a false factual presupposition: such commands are inoperative.

Unfortunately, it is not clear that all moral propositions are imperatives. Even so, I think that we all adhere in practice to one or another form of the semantical criterion. Consider the factual proposition that all unsupported bodies fall. Someone may not believe this to be true, e.g., he may believe in the existence, or at least the possibility, of levitation. If he is able to produce a genuine case of levitation, we should have to give up the factual proposition, or at least restrict it in some way. But contrast this with any moral proposition, such as, we ought to be considerate to one another. First of all, this cannot be understood as saying that we all *are* considerate to each other, a statement that would be false if there were inconsiderate persons. The sentence is phrased so that each of us may know many inconsiderate persons without it requiring us to suppose our moral belief false. If an inconsiderate person should be found, we would not say "Well, here is an interesting exception," as we would say in the case of a levitating human. We also would not think, as in the other case, that our moral beliefs must be restricted in some way in order to provide for the exception. We do not exempt an individual from the scope of a moral proposition merely because he happens not to satisfy it. If anything, the moral proposition has a special application precisely to those who fail to satisfy it. Briefly, if a factual belief is false, it is up to us to change it. But if a moral belief is "false," we do not surrender it: it is, we might say, up to those who fail to live up to the moral proposition to change.

It is feasible that there should be moral propositions that are *nowhere* exemplified and *everywhere* contravened. They would be part of a visionary morality, too demanding, perhaps, to be lived by, given human weaknesses. Yet, there would be nothing irrational in holding such a visionary morality, for it is not generally considered irrational but unrealistic to believe that men will change. But there would be something strange, and perhaps even irrational, in holding to a set of factual beliefs that one knew to be nowhere exemplified and

everywhere contravened. Of course, a man may hold a visionary physics. He may be disgusted, as Kepler was, with the fact
that planetary orbits are ellipses rather than circles. But then
he holds a moral belief about the world, about how it *ought* to
be. But this is no longer a factual belief at all. A man can hold
onto a belief that he *knows* is false only if he removes it from
the arena in which truth or falsity are directly relevant. He cannot hold it as a factual belief if he knows it would be false if it
were one. This sentence puzzles philosophers: "I believe it is
raining, but it isn't." The oddness of this sentence does not entail that a man cannot believe what he knows to be false, but
only that he cannot express this fact without it making him
appear odd. In contrast, saying "I believe people ought to be
considerate, but they aren't," is not a revelation of oddity, but
rather a typical remark. Perhaps one *is* capable of believing
what one knows to be false. But I do not think we would call a
man who believed what he knew to be false a rational man. Of
course, this suggests that our notion of rationality constitutes a
sort of moral belief. For we recognize that a man can, though
we hold that he ought not to, believe a proposition he knows
to be false.

The reason for this is plain. A belief is not a mere state of
the mind or of the soul, an inert trait. When a man believes
something, he is disposed, generally, to act in a certain way,
or in certain ways. If I believe my child is in danger, it is not
merely a matter of giving an affirmative answer to the question
whether I believe that she is in danger. My entire mode of behavior is implicated, and all my relevant factual beliefs are ac-
tivated. If I know that she is not in danger, but then act as
though she were, my actions are in disregard of the facts. But
this defeats the entire purpose of having beliefs to begin with.
One belief is as good or as bad as another if we are not going
to let our beliefs be adjusted to the facts as we know them. In
such a case, we no longer would consider truth and falsity as
relevant to our beliefs. But again, it is not clear what it would

mean to hold a belief if one considered truth and falsity no longer relevant to it.

Because we, in drawing the distinction between factual and moral beliefs, make truth and falsity relevant to factual areas and seemingly irrelevant to moral ones, we are more ready to be relativists in regard to moral beliefs than to factual ones. A proposition that is true, for example, is not merely "true for us." It is true in some more objective sense, difficult again as this may be to define. Thus, if we say, "Proposition p is true for us but false for them," we cannot mean that the proposition is both true and false, for that is impossible. What we must mean is that we believe that p is true, and that they do not, or else they disbelieve p. But if this is all we mean, then what does "true for" add to the fact that p is believed? Of course, we might mean that, though we believe p and they do not, they might be right and we wrong, for the truth or falsity of p has not been clearly established. But whether clearly established or not, p is either true or false if it is the kind of belief to which truth or falsity are relevant, and either they are right or we are: for if a proposition is true, then any proposition incompatible with it has to be false. We can still say a false proposition is "true for them"—but this means only that they believe it, and that their belief is false. It is always possible, as we all know very well indeed, to hold false beliefs. But this does not license a relativism in factual beliefs. If a community believes that the sea devours the sun each night, but that another sun emerges from the earth's womb each morning only to be devoured again by the sea, the earth's enemy, then, though the members of the community believe it to be true— and it is in that sense "true for them"—they are merely poetically deluded, for what is true for them is in fact false, and not just "false for us."

With moral beliefs, on the other hand, we feel far less secure in making such claims. In part, this is because there does not seem to be the same kind of direct connection with the objective structure of the world as there is with factual beliefs, and so we have no immediate way of distinguishing between a moral belief being "right for us" and being right-as-such. If the Hindu rejects the eating of the flesh of cattle, or the Muslim the flesh of swine, or most of us the flesh of humans, then these dietary prohibitions are right for those who practice them without it being plain that they are right as such, in some objectively determinate manner. To be sure, people often justify dietary restrictions by appealing to some primitive sanitary instinct—e.g., the ancient Jews noted that rabbits consume their own excrement and so concluded that eating rabbits was unsanitary.—But even if it could be shown that nothing were more nourishing and less contaminating than the flesh of humans, we still would not feel it right to eat humans: nor would this be due merely to the inertia of an old habit, e.g., the Jew who no longer holds to the old laws might still find himself unable to eat pork. Yet asked to justify our persistance in an old practice, can we do no more than say: well, it is wrong for us though, admittedly, not wrong for the African anthropophages?

Does the matter end here? Is there no basis for rational criticism and defense of moral beliefs? Is the mere fact that people do hold a moral belief a sufficient justification, and perhaps the only justification possible, for the beliefs they hold? This becomes a vexing question if we consider once again our spontaneous semantical criterion for distinguishing factual from moral beliefs. If a moral belief is neither true nor false, it then follows that it is logically independent of any factual belief whatever. In that event, there can be no logical connection whatever between our factual and our moral beliefs. Philosophers have often proposed, to use the classroom slogan, that we cannot deduce an "ought" from an "is." Factual beliefs are those that have to do with the world, and so are rendered true or false depending upon how the world is. But moral beliefs are those that concern how we ought to be or how we ought to act. If "oughts" are compatible with any "is" whatever, then in view of this logical hiatus, no amount of factual information, no set of true beliefs, however wide and penetrating, can require in the name of rationality that we ought to do one thing rather than another or that one practice rather than another is morally right. So science—which is the paradigmatic activity for the acquisition and establishment of factual beliefs—is logically impotent for moral guidance; and while our science may be our glory, and immeasurably superior to the science of any other culture that has ever existed, still, nothing follows from this fact regarding the superiority of our morals. As far as factual beliefs are concerned, one morality is as good or as bad as another: which is to say that there is no objective deciding amongst moralities. So all the more do our factual beliefs seem to be anchored to the world, while our moral beliefs are more or less up to us. A man may hold what moral beliefs he does, no matter what he believes regarding the world as such.

These are consequences of our semantical criterion for distinguishing moral from factual beliefs. We could, of course, give up the semantical criterion and hold, either that factual beliefs are neither true nor false or that moral beliefs *are* either true or false. These are not decisions to be lightly made, for I have shown that the distinction is not one made merely in the classroom, but is reflected in our practices, and that in order to make our choice relevant to our lives a considerable revision of practice would have to be made in the interests of consistency. Moreover, I am prepared to argue that our spontaneous distinction is a sound one. Yet, we might, before surrendering to a radical independence of moral and factual beliefs, point out what in fact is implied in our conclusion that our moral beliefs are up to us, so far as the world itself is concerned. I am not implying by this that whatever we believe is justified by the fact that we believe it, or that any belief whatever is justified or would be justified. All we have done (at best) is to suggest that a certain logical pattern of justification is inoperable. We have not eliminated every basis for justification merely through the consideration that factual and moral beliefs are logically independent, or better, that moral propositions are of the wrong sort to be logically dependent upon factual ones, or even, for that matter, trivially independent of them in the way in which two propositions are independent when the truth-value of one is unaffected by another which has no truth-value to begin with.

One reason moral propositions might lie outside the logical reach of factual ones is that they consist in *rules*. A rule, for example, is not something that can be thought of as true or false, though rules may have other properties, such as fairness or unfairness; and they may be antiquated or cruel or pointless or obscure. If moral beliefs have rules as their content, this would explain our spontaneous propensity to distinguish semantically between factual and moral propositions. So suppose we say flatly that a moral proposition does indeed have this form (we distinguish naturally between a belief about morality and a moral belief; a proposition about morality and a moral proposition). A moral belief, let us say, is one in which a given rule is regarded by the holder of the belief as binding upon those who come within its scope. But this quite clearly implies some connection between the moral belief and certain factual ones, if only because the expression "come within its scope" implies some tacitly specified set of conditions that determine when the rule is to be applied. Let us call these the "application conditions" for the rule. These will include the sorts of things I have already referred to by the factual presuppositions of a command. There is, then, at least enough of a connection between a moral and a factual proposition that the former cannot apply when the latter do not hold. I should like now to explore this tie.

It is not difficult to deduce some set of factual beliefs and social practices from any system of moral beliefs held by a group of persons. Consider the Ten Commandments, for an obvious example. It is quite clear that they were issued to a group that believed in God, and perhaps in other gods as well, so long as they were not ranked ahead of God himself. The first commandments would have no application were these beliefs absent. Or they would be empty and only trivially satisfied. The group quite obviously had a family structure, a marriage structure, and some system of property relationships. An orphan does not fall within the scope of a commandment to honor his father and his mother. Without a (certain) form of marriage, adultery is logically impossible: adultery presupposes fornication, but the converse presupposition does not hold true. Theft entails, through the analysis of the concept, taking something, though the converse inference hardly holds, and there could be no theft without property, though physical pre-emption would remain. The commandments, too, presuppose certain traits of human psychology: covetousness, say. Were envy eradicated from moral psychology, the tenth commandment would have no point, or, again, it would be trivially satisfied. Charity implies the existence of the poor as hope implies the absence of certitude: one cannot hope for what one knows will be the case. And so on. It is a fact that such morally charged terms as honesty, thrift, chastity, courage, obedience, and the like, require, if we are to explain their meaning, the elaboration of conditions that must be understood in purely factual terms. So, at least part of the definition of any moral term will consist in factual ones. Philosophers have rightly insisted that the factual content of these concepts does not exhaust their meaning. But it is difficult to suppose the existence of any moral term that would be empty of factual content: morality is, after all, designed for men living in the world, which inevitably presupposes certain facts, or at least certain factual beliefs, regarding the world and men. The word "good" may seem an exception, but hardly so in such compound expressions as "good woman," "good dentist," or "good father."

It is through their factual content and presuppositions that moral terms and propositions may have some purchase on the world, and to understand a moral term or proposition is to understand at least the conditions under which it may be applied. And the necessity of having a moral rule is appreciated even by those who moot the application conditions in the spirit of casuistry, viz., would the rule be binding under this or that condition? Most systems of belief recognize that there are extenuating circumstances under which certain moral rules are temporarily suspended. Consider the Muslim rule that, during the period of Ramadan, one must fast from sunrise to sunset. This would not apply to believers in the Arctic Circle, where strict compliance would entail starvation, which in no sense is the point of the rule. The Chinese philosopher Mencius acknowledged the rule that one is not to touch one's sister-in-law's hand, but he also tartly observed that this does not mean that one ought not pull one's sister-in-law by her hand from the water if she is drowning. The Talmud is an immense repository of extenuations. The conditions for applying moral propositions are necessarily open in order to insure the elasticity that variations in individual circumstance require. Lack of flexibility might mean either that the rules would no longer apply or that their application would cause such hardships that no one could reasonably expect them to be followed. There is no moral belief, however categorical, that would not lose its applicability under certain easily imagined circumstances.

At times there figures amongst the application conditions for a moral proposition a cognitive condition: a rule is binding upon a man only if he knows the rule. And if, as seems reasonable to assume, knowledge implies understanding, then a rule is binding upon a man only if he understands the terms under which it might apply. This means that the factual content of the relevant moral proposition must be accessible to him. I suppose it would follow that only those moral beliefs whose factual bases would be available everywhere and always to men could be regarded as universal. Such propositions would include those whose application conditions take into account certain traits of men that have always been understood, regardless of place, cultural circumstance, or historical period. But it would be pointless to expect men to be bound by moral rules whose application conditions were unavailable to them, say because the knowledge presupposed were unavailable. So far as these men's understanding of the world differs from that presupposed for a given set of moral propositions, then the propositions can hardly be regarded as binding upon them. A common set of moral beliefs must presuppose a common set of factual beliefs, for differences in factual understanding inevitably penetrate the application conditions for, and hence the understanding of, the moral beliefs themselves. So we are automatically constrained to excuse heathens (speaking broadly) and children. So, however difficult it may be, we are constrained to exonerate men who in their lack of understanding commit actions, which if performed by men whose factual beliefs we suppose consonant with our own, would bring upon them the heaviest moral blame. If a man believes that there are witches and that their presence in the world is so dangerous and destructive of human welfare that allowing them to exist is itself morally blameworthy, and he also believes that only through burning them alive can witches be rendered impotent causally, then we might not blame him for burning those he is convinced are witches, though burning a woman is sickening to us. His world is so different from ours that our principles do not apply. Or, he might, in fact, accept all the same moral rules as we, even those that prohibit the burning of women, since his argument would be that witches are not women in the ordinary sense. Whatever the case, a somewhat different evaluation of the same neutrally described actions is called for, depending upon variations in the factual beliefs of those who perform them. And even though our society might regard it as categorically reprehensible to burn women, I wonder if this moral conviction would survive any imaginable transformation of factual belief? Certainly most of the moral quarrels that go on among us can be reduced in some measure to factual disagreements: to differing factual beliefs regarding the physical effects of marijuana; the social consequences of abortion; the intentions of world communism, and the like. I do not say that people would necessarily agree on their moral beliefs the moment they achieved congruity in their factual beliefs: I only say that in some measure moral differences reflect factual ones. Whatever may be the logical connections between factual and moral propositions—and we assume that they are not the desired ones of entailment and deducibility—there is enough of a tie between them, so that when we reckon in the application conditions of moral beliefs, we have some basis for rational criticism and rational debate in the moral sphere.

A *form of life*, as I understand it, is partially defined by a set of moral rules that participants in that form hold as binding upon each other and by a set of factual beliefs, some of which constitute application conditions for the former. Bindingness may be understood as the mechanism through which the form of life is internalized and, hence, as the will-to-power of the totality upon its members. One, then, can hardly enjoin toleration of the moral beliefs of a community without also tolerating their factual beliefs, for the connection is sufficiently delicate between the two sets for us to expect that transformation in the one entails transformation in the other, and, hence, a transformation in the form of life itself. This was tacitly appreciated in a famous episode in China, when one of the missionaries, Father Matteo Ricci, a correspondent of Galileo and a mathematician in his own right, offered to teach the Chinese ministers what he knew of modern science. They would be able to predict eclipses, would be able to do wonderful things! In the end, the ministers decided it would be better not to know these things. For theirs was a form of life that had worked well enough for a very long time, and surely the most that can be asked of a form of life is that it can be lived, that it bestows a degree of rationality upon existence, and that it holds chaos at bay. It is difficult for us to sympathize with these mandarins, since we regard knowledge as liberating. We regard them in somewhat the same light as we view those astronomers at Padua who failed to look into Galileo's telescope. Yet I believe we might appreciate this refusal to acknowledge facts in pragmatic terms. A system that induces rationality is through that fact alone of considerable value. One does not, in science any more than in life, lightly surrender a system of beliefs that facilitates experience, that renders it tractable and smooth. In science we see this conservatism operating in a natural way: scientists introduce all sorts of auxilliary hypotheses in order to explain away discrepancies with theory, simply because it is easier to do this than to jettison a theory and surrender the rationality it has brought into life. It is as though any theory were better than none. Only when the discrepancies become too great, or when the auxiliary hypotheses render the theory itself too unwieldy for it to function properly is there reform or revision. Even then, the old theory is retained until a new one is ready. So if the Paduan scoffers had confidence in their own theories, they had confidence in their powers of explaining away the phenomena Galileo pretended to have discovered, and perhaps explaining them away easily, say through citing optical imperfections. And much the same thing may be said of morality. People are bound to revolutionize their form of life when they discover that the factual beliefs anchoring their moral beliefs to the world have shored away, leaving the latter no point of attachment to the world. The old Chinese were right in predicting what would happen if they accepted the new knowledge that was offered them. Forms of life have died as Western beliefs have swept the world. Merely preaching a different morality, however, is unlikely to alter a practice. But changes of heart may come through changes in mind.

Philosophers who have emphasized the gap between facts

and values, who have insisted that values have no place in the world of fact, often make an invidious comparison between moral and factual disagreements. With factual disagreement, they have argued, one may, in principle, state the requirements for resolving the disagreement in a rational way. Matters are not the same with moral disagreements. And indeed they are not. But to a degree, if the relationships I have been discussing hold, they suggest that one way to resolve moral disagreement is through the resolving factual ones. We refute a moral proposition by demonstrating its inapplicability.

Although a group's factual beliefs offer us some basis for criticizing their moral beliefs, they do not in the same sense offer us a basis for establishing any moral beliefs or for deciding between different sets of moral beliefs, provided, if that were possible, we hold all the same factual beliefs. We can, through the removal of false factual beliefs, render certain moral beliefs inapplicable. But we cannot in the same way ever decisively justify their application. Or rather: any moral belief based on a factual belief is applicable if the latter is true. But incompatible moral beliefs can in principle have just the same factual basis. It may be pointed out, in compensation, that we have roughly the same situation within the domain of factual beliefs. Thus it is a problem for inductivists that any number of theories may be compatible with all the same observations, though incompatible with one another. We may through observation decisively falsify a theory. But we cannot in the same manner decisively establish such a theory or differentiate between competing theories having the same observational basis. And just as we cannot deduce an 'ought' from an 'is', so we cannot induce a theoretical 'is' from an observational one. This may be taken to suggest, both in the domains of factual and of moral theory, that there is an inexpungeable creative leap, that a system of moral beliefs, like a theoretical system in science, is the imposition of a certain structure upon the world. These structures are only negatively controlled by the facts. If our factual beliefs are false, if our observational sentences are false, then our moral beliefs and our factual theories have, respectively, no application.

Knowledge cannot tell us what we ought to do or what we theoretically ought to believe. It only tells us that when certain factual beliefs have proven false we cannot consistently and sincerely act upon and believe in them. We must then find new bases for our theories and our moralities. Logically we can always do this, but it involves a measure of creativity. The asymmetry between criticism and establishment is one with which we simply must live.

Now, it is against the controlling background of their factual beliefs that I should like to discuss some of the moral beliefs of the Oriental peoples. These are beliefs, the application of which logically presuppose the truth of certain factual beliefs; and if these beliefs prove false, then the moral beliefs as formulated can have no application, can have no point of purchase upon the world. It is open always, in such cases, for men to continue in their practices—it is not a moral belief if it does not go with a practice—but men can no longer justify their practices as they could have done when they did not know their factual beliefs were false. They would need a different basis altogether.

The Indians, in whom I shall chiefly be interested, have always prized factual knowledge, and they have prized it in a manner and for a reason close to the spirit of my inquiry. They have not been concerned with knowledge as an ornament of existence or for its own sake, but rather they have appreciated it in thoroughly practical terms. In this they were like the Greeks. Socrates over and over again impugns abstract, ornamental, disinterested knowledge. The point and purpose of our acquiring knowledge is to live better lives. Socrates held the interesting theory that one could not know and not do the morally right thing, so that if men do evil, it is always through ignorance. There are obvious discrepancies with this: it is a characteristic feature of moral life that men know what is the right thing and are unable to do it, or know what is the wrong thing and are unable not to do it. These phenomena came to be the center of considerable attention in ancient moral psychology, under the heading of the weakness, or paralysis, of the will. Socrates' original theory appears to have been as follows: It is not in the nature of men to know what is good and not to apply this knowledge. Nor could they misapply it. Knowledge itself can, of course, be misapplied or misused. A surgeon can use his knowledge as easily to damage as to benefit his patients. Socrates, however, could not see how knowledge of the Good could be misused: that we could make a bad use of such knowledge. It seemed inconsistent to suppose that knowledge of the good could have a bad use and, hence, a misapplication; and it followed, then, that if men did misuse knowledge, it could not be knowledge of the *good* that they were misusing. In general, if men misuse anything, it is because they lack knowledge of the good, and so the evil men do is caused by ignorance alone. Knowledge of the good, therefore, leads inevitably to right action. But there is a difference between *misapplication* and *inapplication*, and while it may be impossible or at least paradoxical to suppose that knowledge of the good can be abused, it need not follow that having the knowledge compels us to put it to use. So, one is led to postulate an intervening, applicative mechanism, the will, which must, in the psychology of Plato's *Republic*, function in support of reason if reason is to dominate our lives. To paraphrase Immanuel Kant, reason without will is as impotent as will without reason is blind.

It is instructive to compare the Indian conception of knowledge with this classical one, instructive if only because, as we shall see, the will is not anything like the important moral concept in the East that it is in the West. Equally, there is none of the agony over freedom of the will, which is, after all, the paradigmatic philosophical concern in the Western tradition.

Once again, the Indian conceives of knowledge in practical terms, as leading directly to felicity. But knowledge is not, as with Socrates, specifically individuated with regard to its object, viz., the Good, but rather it is seen as the product of a certain kind of transformation. It is what is left when false beliefs are removed. Here, I think, there is no need for a notion of applying knowledge, for by the time one has knowledge, the transformation in question has been achieved. In effect, one does not have to *do* anything at all, and, hence, there is no reason for the will to operate. This sounds exotic and abstract, perhaps, so let me hasten to furnish an analogy from common experience that satisfies this description almost to perfection. The experience I have in mind consists in the removal of an illusion.

Consider, to use a typical Indian example, the case of a man who sees that what he perceived and feared to be a snake, was all along only a length of rope that he *took* for a snake. When he sees it for what it is, he cannot any longer believe nor act on the belief that it is a snake. And either his fear must immediately dissipate, or else the fear would not really have been caused by its seeming object—a snake—to begin with. If he remains afraid of the rope, knowing it for what it is, his fear is abnormal, for fear of pieces of rope is not a normal fear, but a fetish. If, again, a man continues to act towards the rope as though it were a snake, he remains in the grip of an illusion. The answer to the question "What shall I do about the snake?" is "Nothing." Instead you must learn to see it for what it is. In other words, to see the world right is to remove the need for an action that makes sense only in terms of a set of beliefs that are now seen as false.

This case is an interesting one for a number of reasons. First, to us it suggests a common analogy in psychotherapeutic theory. When a neurotic's fears are due to false beliefs, namely, the kinds of beliefs a child could have, then to rectify the beliefs is to eliminate the fear; and if the fear persists after the beliefs have been rectified, this means only that we have not really rectified the beliefs. For knowledge here has to be liberating. We do not, so to speak, have to apply the knowledge, for in effect there is nothing to apply it to: the situation that seemed to call for action has simply disappeared in the course of removing the illusion. Secondly, the knowledge in question here is not simply another fact to add to the facts we may have gathered in a life's accumulation of information. It is something we live through: it is, to use a fashionable term, existential. It is a living through of what seems to be a transformation of the world but is really only a transformation of the manner in which one sees the world, and, so is a transformation of oneself. A man could, of course, always believe that there really had been a snake, which was replaced by a piece of rope at the critical moment. This would be a magical and primitive belief, the rather more scientific belief in illusions being an intellectual advance of considerable proportions. The important aspect here is that in the course of transformation nothing happens to the world.

The experience of living through an illusion bears some resemblance to what it must be to sustain a religious conversion. One sees after all just the same trees, just the same stones. But, without there being any objective transformation in the field of experience, one sees them now as laden with divine meaning. Or, to take a more familiar case, it is like learning to read: the meaningless marks that one has seen for so long are given a meaning. It is the same and different at once, but the difference is due to a modification of understanding rather than an alteration in the world. When the whole world is seen as different from what one had believed it to be then the rules and theories applicable to *that* world no longer have application. When beliefs are revealed as illusory, when the scales have fallen from our eyes, then our problems and our data for attacking them are alike relegated to the illusory world we have discarded and we begin afresh.

When the snake gives way to the rope, the principles worked out for coping with snakes are not invalidated as such, but merely put out of play. If again, to use another Indian example, the piece of silver that two men struggle towards turns out to be a piece of mother of pearl instead, the lusts and the mechanisms for coping with the lusts of men are not invalidated, but put out of play. They belong to situations that do not really hold. Imagine now that the whole world should turn out to have been a vast illusion! Then it is not as though there were something, that I took for something else, but as though there were nothing, which I took to be something. If the whole world is delusion and dream, then the problems that bear upon the world and our conduct in it have no ultimate application. The radical solution to the question: "What ought we to do in the world?" is: there is no world in which we can, much less ought to, do one thing rather than another. And if in the end my concern is how I shall gain release from the grip of the world—and this, as we shall see, is the practical question that has obsessed Indian philosophers and which their philosophies have almost invariably attempted to answer—then the radical answer is that there is no world from whose grip release is wanted or needed. To see this is to see the pointlessness of the concern. The release from the thirst for release comes when we see that that from which we sought release was an illusion. If it is an illusion, so is release one.

These are audacious, heady thoughts, and they take us rather far ahead of our story. I mention them prematurely because they illustrate the extraordinary role that knowledge came to play in the economy of Indian thought. Through knowledge, the Indian hoped to find deliverance from the class of problems we more commonly suppose knowledge will help us to solve. Knowledge in India was pragmatic and therapeutic but curiously unconcerned with the immediate problems of life or with simple solutions to these problems. The Indian wanted a total radical solution to the problem of life as such, and he was interested in nothing less—he would accept nothing intermediate between everything and nothing. We can appreciate it only if we also appreciate certain factual beliefs, antecedently held and hardly seriously questioned, regarding the world itself. If, to put it bluntly, these beliefs are false, then the solution to the problems they give rise to are no longer interesting, except as curious products of the human mind: they are not invalidated but only rendered inoperative. And this returns us to our immediate concerns.

The foundations of Indian philosophy, metaphysical as well as moral, and of Indian moral attitude and practice, are made up of a set of astonishing factual beliefs. It is fair to say that for some centuries these beliefs have not been submitted to the sort of criticism that the factual bases, or alleged factual bases, of Western morality have endured. It is a factual belief, after all, that we are children of God and that our moral codes were handed us by God. Western morality has—though this may be a short-run assessment—proved fairly resilient. The theological bases have, in many instances, dissolved without bringing down the entire moral edifice that they were supposed to justify. Perhaps that only shows that men had represented the foundations of their morality incorrectly. Be this as it may, I do not believe I exaggerate in saying that if the factual beliefs of India to which I refer are false, there is very little point in Indian philosophy, and very little room for serious application of Indian moral beliefs except so far as the latter be *faute de mieux*.

I am not saying these beliefs are false. I am only saying that they are factual beliefs and so are either true or false. How to show that they are either true or false would be very difficult to do, and perhaps could not be done at all. In this respect they are immune to criticism except insofar as we might regard immunity to criticism as exactly the most fatal sort of vulnerability factual beliefs may sustain. But that carries me considerably beyond the task I have set myself.

2

Karma AND CASTE

Indian tradition recognizes six orthodox *darshanas*, or philosophical systems. A system is considered orthodox if it accepts the Vedic corpus as revelation. One of the traditional schools, the *Mimamsa*, seems at first glance less a philosophical system than a systematic technique of scriptural interpretation. Thus, it begins as an attempt to rationalize the Vedic corpus, to classify the mass of hymns and prayers and ritualistic instruction of which it is composed, in such a way as to provide some system of duties and injunctions that may serve as a guide in life. Such a task must always be performed when there is a body of revelation not conspicuously consistent or even coherent, expecially if it is to be applied fundamentalistically as a moral-legal code. But this concern very quickly leads one to reflect on the correctness of an interpretation and, thence, to a general inquiry concerning the general conditions for obtaining reliable knowledge. Thus, in the end, *Mimamsa* becomes a school of speculative epistemology. By contrast, *Nyaya* was from the beginning specifically concerned with questions of logic and inference—it was in fact a school of what we today would call analytical philosophy—but its analysis never became independent of the brooding concerns of Hindu religious speculation. Nyaya thus remained orthodox, offering schemes of liberation and salvation. Philosophical and religious concerns are inextricably intermingled in the densely knotted fabric of Indian thought. And since nothing was considered more practical than the attainment of salvation, in its own terms Indian thought, however rarified, never became abstract, disinterested, or irrelevant.

The array of philosophical systems includes three main heterodox, or *nastika*, schools. They are heterodox solely because of their attitude towards the Vedas, which are not counted as revelation by them. These systems are Jainism, Buddhism, and Carvaka, or Materialism. Only the latter appears to express a philosophical position as such, at least by Western criteria. But Buddhist writings contain some of the most sophisticated philosophical writings in Eastern, or any, literature. Jainism, which we know as a religion of extraordinary austerity, was not philosophically retrograde either. In fact no system of thought that was not philosophically athletic could have survived in the gymnastic atmosphere of Indian dialectics. But neither could any purely secular philosophical system have survived. For the heterodox systems were no less theologically obsessed than their orthodox rivals, and the orthodox systems were no more protected from the obligation to find sharp philosophical arguments than the heterodox alternatives. Philosophy and religion were never separate enterprises nor independent concerns.

This suggests two features of Indian thought. It suggests, to begin with, that knowledge and clear reasoning were held to play overwhelmingly important roles in the achievement of essentially religious goals. As we have already seen implied, knowledge was not regarded as one of several means but as the best means to salvation, so much so that it is often difficult to distinguish salvation from the possession of knowledge as such. Irrationalisms, as avenues of religious success, were unremittingly combatted and disregarded in favor of cognitive analysis, which remained ascendant. Secondly, the Indians' preoccupation with salvation lent an urgency to philosophical acuity, which prevented philosophy either from becoming self-oriented and frivolous (as is its tendency when separated from extraphilosophical obligations) or from developing into an independent system of abstract conceptual inquiry. Nevertheless, it became extraordinarily subtle, and the Indian philosophers became masters of refined distinction. Since knowledge was the avenue to salvation, failure of knowledge meant the abortion of redemption. Just as in the great Scholastic period of Western philosophy, when any slight misstep could bring heresy and damnation, finesse in framing distinctions becomes second nature. It is only when the price for crudeness becomes small that philosophy can afford the sort of logical shoddiness we find, say, in nineteenth century Western thought, when men did not need to be sharp for extra-worldly reasons, and philosophy as a discipline had not yet attained professionalization. For these reasons, however, in India as in the High Middle Ages, philosophy tended to be increasingly concerned with minute and rarefied distinctions, which served to inhibit freer, more spontaneous speculations and bold, drastic simplifications. Thought seems inevitably to turn into prescribed channels when philosophy is made specifically pragmatic and where the price for error is made too high to expect anyone to have to pay it. Indian philosophy was forced to become a mental gymnasium by its own inner logic, and in it logical virtuosity becomes routinized and practitioners, professionals— an insider's game, so to speak, where conciseness and acuity made its propositions virtually inaccessible, even to the literate outsider. It is effectively hermetic and sealed, much in the way in which professional mathematical writing is today to even the well-informed and disciplined lay person.

At this point it may be wondered, if knowledge is either a necessary condition for salvation or if it is salvation as such, and if the achievement of knowledge demands so rigorous a schooling, what hope can there be of salvation for the plain dull mortal, unequipped and possibly unequipable with the technical apparatus and the sharpness demanded for applying it? Certainly, the theory appears to restrict salvation to a class of intellectuals, and in terms of Indian social structure, to members of the Brahman caste. For they were the ones uniquely qualified by birth (and admission to the Brahman caste is only through birth) to serve as religious technicians, that is, to perform the duties and enact the rituals specified in the Vedas, and so alone were in the position to study the relevant texts and to profit by the exegetical disciplines. Obviously, if only Brahmans are in a position to be saved, and if none can become a Brahman except by birth, then non-Brahmans cannot be saved unless—and this is the curious alternative seized upon by Indian theorists—they can manage to *get reborn as Brahmans!*

Now we are familiar with this mode of thought in our own religious tradition. The religious convert is submitted to some *rite de passage* and so is born anew, vested with a fresh identity. He is told that "Except ye be born again, ye cannot enter the Kingdom." One of Christ's auditors, in the St. John Gospel, finds this a puzzling and impossible proposition. Is he being asked, at his advanced age, to re-enter and then re-exit his mother's literal womb? This strikes him as alike difficult and silly: surely nothing quite so messy and undignified can be the sole entry condition for the Kingdom of God! And Christ's iteration convey the point that something spiritual rather than obstetrical was meant. Christ does *not* mean something metaphorical rather than something literal: it is a real rebirth of the soul rather than a mythic rebirth of the body which baptisms and *rites de passages* achieve. There is nothing mythic, in the eyes of believers, in the transubstantiation of bread into flesh: it is a miracle that really transpires, not the poetic simulation of a mutation that one would merely like to see happen. The rite does not represent rebirth: it is precisely through it that rebirth literally occurs. One emerged a new person, with a fresh identity and a new name. For the Hindu, however, rebirth is not in the same sense a voluntary transport, attained through the mediation of effective ceremony, conspicuous only to the eyes of faith. It is a prosaic and routine occurence, as common as birth and death. Each birth is a rebirth, in fact, the literal re-embodiment of a self sundered from its most recent body in its latest death.

This is the doctrine of metempsychoses. It is a belief held in common by all the orthodox Indian schools, and, with one exception, by the heterodox schools as well. Buddhists, who argued against the existence of souls or selves, obviously could not accept metempsychoses as the explicit reimplantation of an old soul in a new body. But nevertheless Buddhists accepted a form of transmigration. I am, according to them, identical with myself through all my past and future incarnations. It is only that this is not to be explained with reference to the perdurance of a self-identical entity, viz., the soul or self, from lifetime to lifetime. I shall attempt later to analyze the Buddhist teaching on this matter. Their theory was that we are held together, and go from lifetime to lifetime by means of something called *craving*, without it following that there is something that does or has the craving: it is craving without a craver, if we may temporarily put it so. But while rejecting the theory of migrating souls that was the orthodox teaching, Buddhists accepted the phenomenon of transmigration as a brute fact of the universe. It is essential to the understanding of Buddhist thought, ethical and otherwise, as it is essential to understanding the entire complexion of philosophical positions in India, that we appreciate that everyone supposed it a fact of the universe that transmigration occurs everywhere and always, not just to some of us but to all of us, over and over again. It is a factual belief, but a factual belief that has immense moral and metaphysical implications. Without implicit reference to it, we cannot make sense of much that we must understand.

In theory at least, Hinduism is not a proselytizing religion. It is not, because the only way in which one can become a Hindu is by the avenue of direct birth. So salvation is in principle accessible to all, though not directly. One must be born first a Hindu and then a Hindu of the right sort, in order to achieve it. This is not something beyond our powers since we have a say in our ultimate destinies. The belief in metempsychoses—or metemsomatosis, as some regard it more fittingly designated—is not a rare belief as such. In one or another form, it may be encountered the world over. In Hinduism, however, it is associated with a quite distinctive retributive theory, *karma*, according to which the body and station in life we next acquire is exactly determined by our conduct in our present body and station in life. Transmigration is not a random matter; we are able to a nice degree to predict, and hence to a measure control, our rebirths. By fit conduct in this life, I can assure a sociosomatic improvement or promotion in the next. Or I can assure, by misconduct, a proportionate demotion in the scale of things.

Karma works in a purely automatic manner, like the mechanisms of genetics. There is no mythology of a recording angel, no last judgment in which our good and evil deeds are counterweighed. No, the karmic system is, as it were, a moral mechanics, with a predetermined output for any given input. I have, of course, no control over what I am in my present life, and have no real control over the sociosomatic conditions within which I am constrained to behave. No fundamental improvement is to be expected in this life. But the way I am situated here is exactly the result of choices I made in an earlier life, and I have only borne the karmic inheritance of those choices. Therefore, I have only myself to blame or to congratulate for what I am. Determinists like Clarence Darrow enjoyed saying that since we have no control over our character and circumstances, we cannot claim free will. But the karmic theory puts me precisely in a position to choose my character and circumstances in a next life, and, in effect, to have chosen them in this one as well. Each of us decides whether he is to rise or fall in the stratified universe. By evil deeds I can sink even beneath the human stratum into animal domains and worse. Or, I can rise to the station of twice-born brahmahood and beyond: I can become a godling or a god. Not even the gods are exempt from *karma*, for by accumulated demerits they can fall as far as anyone, only to have to begin again the tedious ascent. We cannot escape *karma*, and insofar as *karma* is a fact of existence, ethical differences are in large measure factually based. The strata of karmic ascent and descent are not merely social conventions, but stained into the basal fabric of the world. Social distinctions are as ultimate as any distinctions there are.

All, or almost all actions bear karmic fruit; and in pursuit of the ends of life, I cannot avoid an ultimate retributive karmic accumulation, which I shall bear in my next embodiment. The karmically relevant actions are those that belong to what is recognized as the *trivarga*, or "group of three," which I shall refer to as *trivargic* actions. These are the three secular ends of life that Hinduism acknowledges as legitimate: *dharma*, or duty; *artha*, or wealth; and *kama*, or pleasure, usually understood as sexual pleasure, or *volupté*. The pursuit of these various ends was, in consequence of the karmic overtones, subject to a remarkable degree of codification. Very little room was left for spontaneity: the hindu was obliged to calculate his usages carefully, with always a sharp eye for the karmic price attached to each trivargic act. The celebrated *Kama Sutra* is a comically codified manual of erotic engineering, with precise instructions for the kind of cry appropriate for each degree of ecstasy. The recent wave of sexual anxiety that has overtaken us in the West has an Eastern precedent, where there was, in addition, the depressing contrast drawn between human powers and those of the gods, whose sexual virtuosity trespassed into miracle.

In addition to trivargic acts, there are non-karmic or even contra-karmic acts, which pertain to a fourth end of life in the traditionally prescribed scheme. This is *moksha*, or liberation, which must be appreciated, as we shall see, primarily as liberation from *karma*. Generally, it was not considered fitting for a man to concentrate upon *moksha*. Rather, there is a stage of life in which a man ought seriously to pursue it. Hindus traditionally counted four main stages, or *ashramas*, in the well-ordered life: a well-lived life would find a man, after having been student, householder, and businessman; having done his duty, amassed his fortune, and attained sexual fulfillment; and at the end of his life withdrawn from the world's demands; in a final period of religious exercise, questing for release from the hooks of *karma*. Poetic and dramatic literature is rich in evocations of the peaceful jungle hermitage to which, after the rigors of worldly life, men might retire at last, having severed the ties of love and commitment that bound them to the world, pilgrims athirst for a final severance. The Hindu conception of a whole life is certainly admirable: it suggests a balance and lack of fanaticism in the pursuit of any end to the detriment or expense of all the others. It is understandable that one of the trivargic actions should act as a counterweight to the others: men do go overboard in the chase for wealth and pleasure, and even in the blue-stockinged lopsided cultivation of rectitude. That the appetite for *moksha* should require counterweight and regulation, however, is not part of standard human psychology, and it will require some special attention, though the explanation is not hard to find. Power and pleasure are universal drives. So in a way is duty, for no one can be a member of a society without internalizing a concept of duty, and once internalized, it becomes a drive as well. But *karma* is a local concept, and without reference to it, we cannot so much as frame the idea of *moksha*.

At this point I must introduce a complicating feature of the karmic theory, that of caste. It is with reference to caste that the specific notions of *dharma* holding in India must be appreciated. There are four traditional castes, with the *Brahman* caste generally conceded as supreme. Next comes the *Kshatriya*, who are the military and the temporal ruling class. After

that come the *Vaisya*, the professional and artisan class, and finally the *Sudra*, or *Shudra*, the laboring caste. This tetradic division has divine sanction, inasmuch as the four castes were
recognized in one of the Rig Veda hymns, the *Purusha-
Shukta*, which explains the provenance of the castes from various portions of some cosmic person: *Brahman, Kshatriya,
Vaisya,* and *Sudra* issue respectively from the head, heart,
loins, and feet of this Person. This very naturally suggests an
isomorphism between individuals and social structures—
microcosm and macrocosm—roughly along lines envisioned
in the *Republic* of Plato. That the etiology of social castes is
accepted as revelation is an uncomfortable reminder that Plato
hoped to get his citizens to accept a Noble Lie, which in turn
would make palatable social divisions and personal situations
they might otherwise find unsupportable. He hoped they would
believe that the three main classes—rulers, auxiliaries, and
the masses—sprang from various ores of decreasing nobility,
which, although they have a common mother, the Earth, to
whom they owe filial allegiance, gives a natural, and indeed an
inevitable, explanation of people's individual stations in life. In
any event, as in Plato, the Hindu scheme has room for any
number of parallels between psychic and social welfare. Plato
saw his three castes as corresponding respectively to the reason, will, and appetite in the individual psyche. The Hindus
make a correspondence rather with soul, intellect, mind, and
body, in descending order. And these, in turn, are mapped
onto the four *purusharthas* we have considered: *moksha,
dharma, kama,* and *artha*. So the *Brahman* are the soul of society and concerned with *moksha;* the Kshatriya the heart of
society and concerned with duty; etc. Interestingly, wealth is
associated with labor and with the lowest caste status. Officially, the other ends of life are higher, which is characteristic
of aristocratic systems, most of which tend to romantic orderings of human values.

One can see in all of this the basis for any number of bad arguments that favor invidious social distinctions. Thus, we can virtually hear people arguing: just as there are four parts to the person, just as there are four elements, and just as there are four ends of life, so there must be four—no more and no fewer—social castes. Western political history is rich in such appeals to the harmony of structures, e.g., just as the body has a head, so must the state; and just as the head rules the body, so the king must rule the state. We can be hypnotized by such reasonings. Even were everything else impeccable, this would justify at best the existence of four castes, not the existence of castes as such. And, in fact the harmonic analogies are merely mischievous masqueraders for sound reasoning. Imagine that there are a hundred great ideas, as Mortimer Adler maintains, and only ninety-six elements. Ought we to set scientists looking for the missing four elements, or ought we to suppose instead that some of the ideas are reducible to others, so that really there are only ninety-six? And how do we rationalize the existence of only fifty states with any of this? And only nine Beethoven symphonies? Apologists for the Indian system like to point out that after all, some men are more suited to turn the soil than to administer, and others are more suited to design churches than to preach in them: the best system is that in which, each man doing his "thing," each man can fulfill himself and society can attain its ends simultaneously and harmoniously. Plato felt injustice consisted in crossing the lines, which is both socially disastrous and individually distorting. In reality, however, castes are not composed of individuals uniquely suited to the ideally prescribed caste functions; *Brahmans* may be cooks and office workers, even hand laborers, as readily as priests. The contingencies of genetics and economics swamp such tidy schemes.

In the ideal scheme, a person can, by scrupulously following the duty prescribed to his caste, expect a progressive betterment of his station in subsequent embodiments. Our *karma* will promote our caste-standing and, given the system of correspondences, our individual standing as well. This is sublimely suggested in the *Bhagavad Gita*, whose ideas I shall later analyze. Apart from this, there is little doubt that society as a whole would flourish if rulers, workers, artisans, and guides, performed their duty exactly and efficiently—though this presupposes a fairly stable social order, one to be maintained rather than modified in directions of social justice, and it has a pessimistic overtone if it be adopted as an argument in favor of castes, for the harmony of society would shatter if everyone were *Brahman*. It is dismal to reflect that there must always be enough people whose *karma* is evil if any work is to be done. But these are sophistries. The fact is that there are vastly more than the four traditional castes, the array of castes being so complex and ramified that any persisting belief in harmonic correspondences in Nature must make us shrink before the physical chaos this must mean. However, the sole criterion for karmic advancement is not merely adherence to the immemorial *dharma* of one's caste.

Superstition throws a wide shadow across the caste system, for members of a lower caste can pollute members of a higher one in such a way as to insure a detrimental karma for them. A merely passing *Sudra* can inadvertently pollute a *Brahman* and, thereby, retard or degrade the latter's karmic situation. We can be but little concerned here with the apparatus of pollution, which is exceedingly important in Indian life, although less so now than formerly. Certain practices are polluting, certain substances are polluting, certain occupations are polluting—those occupations that bring one into contact with polluting substances, e.g., a laundress must wash clothes, but clothes bear the stains of the body, which are polluting. Naturally, there have to be mechanisms of purification to counteract pollution, and given human credulity, the systematization of pollution and purification become magical practices usurping the austere values of *dharma* as agencies of *karma*, and the whole structure becomes overgrown with a jungle prodigality of taboos, purgatives, rituals, and charms, all of which serve as prophylactics against one's karmic degradation. Social and moral energies increasingly get drawn into activities whose sole purpose is to keep the castes from mutual contamination and to rationalize practices that have application only on the basis of belief in pollution and in *karma*.

It is easy for us to be scornful of such beliefs. They probably originated in sanitary precautions, as many prohibitions doubtless do. But in an age where effective alternatives are available to guard against the illnesses these crude efforts at sanitation originally protected men from, the practices have been energized to an extent hardly proportionate to their original practical purpose, should they, in fact, have had any. It is difficult for us to appreciate them, much in the same way as it is difficult for us to see through a fetishist's eyes, to respond with the same excitement and emotion to what, for us, is a bit of cloth or a mundane garment. I am not concerned, however, with criticizing the pollution practices of India as such. Their specific content notwithstanding, they may have served an integrative role in Indian society, and so may be obliquely justified on functional grounds. I am interested only in emphasizing the extent to which they complicate the karmic theory. To begin with, a life is not, after all, the result of one's actions in prior lives. It is also a matter of the degree to which a person may have become polluted, even inadvertently, in various passages. Secondly, the omnipresent threat of pollution in conjunction with the variegated circumstances in which pollution may be transmitted cannot but have served to discourage karmic ambitions. The chances of ascent through right living, which is in itself taxing, becomes increasingly remote. And so the pessimistic cast of the Indian mind—we have hardly touched upon this—is reinforced.

The compartmentalization of mankind into castes has caused it to be divided into so many species between which there is no possibility of fraternizing. One cannot marry members of another caste nor, for that matter, eat with them. The members of a different caste are, in effect, members of a different *species:* the distinction between castes is roughly the same as the distinction we recognize between humans and animals. We do not marry with animals, nor are we called upon to fraternize with them. We have a different ethic for dealing with animals than we have for dealing with one another. And apart from avoidance prohibitions, nothing in India ever was worked out that could serve as a general ethic overarching the differences between castes, treating men, as it were, as equals in some ways. This is very well put by Max Weber in *The Religion of India:*

> *There is no universally valid ethic, but only a strict status compartmentalization of private and social ethic, disregarding the few general and ritualistic prohibitions (particularly the killing of cows). This was of great moment. The doctrine of karma deduced from the principle of compensation for previous deeds in the world, not only explained the caste organization but the rank order of divine, human, and animal beings of all degree. Hence it provided for the coexistence of different ethical codes for different status groups which not only differed widely but were often in sharp conflict . . . [Men] were as unlike as man and animal.*

To be sure, the failure to establish a system of ethics that is held to be universally valid has its compensations. It leads to a measure of toleration. We tolerate the differences between animals and men largely because we regard them as irremediable. If we believed in gods we might similarly regard the differences in conduct between them and us. This rational toleration across species is ubiquitous in India, where different castes count as disjoint ontological orders (and animals and gods are in the same stratification). So, at the very least, the Indian system must be described as nonfraternal. Moreover, Indian toleration, however commendable as such, rests upon a set of factual beliefs that are at best disputable.

Let me comment upon this for a moment. Mere toleration of differences has a limit. The limit is drawn by the differences we are called upon to tolerate. Some differences we cannot tolerate and at the same time hold any moral beliefs at all. An Indian will always excuse the actions of a man belonging to a different caste if it is provided for in the moral beliefs that belong to and define the man's caste, even though they are proscribed by his own caste, just as the fact that something is done by an animal or by a god is always an excusing condition. Imagine, for example, that there is a caste of thieves. There is honor amongst them, to be sure. But are we required to tolerate them on the mere grounds that they are thieves? There is no basis for moral discussion whatever if there is no sense of everyone belonging to the same general community within which differences may be tolerated. We have already noted the possibility of ultimate moral differences. And it could be that the differences between castes would be of this sort. But this will not serve. That the difference between two moral systems could be based on a difference between two types of individual depends upon our antecedent willingness to accept this essentially factual belief as true. And it scarcely is obvious that it is true.

The general notion of justice may be negatively defined. People under the same set of conditions should be treated differently only if the differences between them can be considered relevant to the difference in treatment. This means that men should be treated equally in the same or similar circumstances when there is no difference between them that would justify a difference in treatment. And this, I think, must be appreciated in factual or causal terms. Thus, if two students turn in similar papers, but written in different colored inks, I should be acting unjustly if I should grade one higher than the other, since there is no obvious causal connection between the quality of the paper and the color of ink in which it is written: the difference is there, but causally irrelevant. So, for the matter, would be the sex or race differences between the writers. In other words, the fact that differences exist does not entail differential treatment unless the differences are causally relevant.* It is the same in science. Galileo once considered the theory that Babylonians could cook eggs by whirling them in slings round their heads. We cannot do this, he found; and since their eggs and slings were the same, the difference must be, he jokingly suggests, that *they* were Babylonians and *we* are not. But of course there is no relevant difference here. Our concept of universality in science is the twin to our concept of universality in justice. And it is this that the caste system prohibited from evolving in India.

The principle of universality does not mean that men are to be treated alike, but only that they can justifiably be treated differently only when the differences between them are causally relevant. Indeed, it is consistent with this principle that treating men alike when there is a causally relevant difference between them could constitute an injustice. It is not just to an individual to appoint him to a job for which he is not suited, or to make him part of a team when he is not qualified to do the work. But apart from that, mere equal treatment of all, granting that it avoids injustices of one sort, leaves open the question of the level at which they are to be treated: we can treat all men as lords or as swine, and either way avoid the injustices due to inequity. It was specifically as a safeguard

---

* If we have two individuals, equally qualified for a job which only one of them can have, there is no rational basis for preferring one over the other. Either we must continue to press for some factual differentiation, or resort to some wholly random basis for choice, e.g., tossing a fair coin a fair number of times. What would be unjust would be to pass from relevant to irrelevant differences. A difference is irrelevant when no causal basis exists for supposing it would serve to make one a better occupant for the job than the other.

against this that the Christian Golden Rule was introduced. Its criterion was whether I would like to be treated in the way in which I treat others: if not, then I ought not treat them in that manner either. If we treated everyone as we ourselves would be treated, then, the implication runs, we would achieve equity at the proper level. But this assumes that the way in which we should want to be treated is the way in which each man would wish to be. If not, then the self-regarding criterion does not operate as it should. Probably it is false. But it does not, I think, lead to the excesses which critics sometimes suppose it does. Thus, the case of the masochist is often cited: if the principle which defines his aberrant taste were generalized, universal pain would be the result. This in fact is not so. The masochist generally does not delight in pain for its own sake. The masochistic fantasy involves moral suffering, with a special emphasis upon degradation and humiliation; e.g., the masochist fantasizes being flagellated by a woman. In his scheme, the woman must be socially inferior to begin with, or there would not be the same kind of delicious humiliation, etc. But the point being made is that his pleasure depends upon others not being treated as he wishes to be: there has to be a dominant agent of his degradation in his universe, or the pleasure vanishes. Much the same considerations apply to sadism. These are perversions that depend upon others not being treated as one is oneself, and so cannot be generalized. But for just this reason, reference to myself, with my special tastes and preferences, is rendered irrelevant in moral generalization. It is not how I would like to be treated, but rather how any arbitrarily chosen individual would have to be treated if there were no basis for arbitrary or invidious treatment. Insofar as the Christian principle involves or entails similar treatment of all, and my own preferences are the key to how all are to be treated, it entails as many injustices as can be imagined: for after all, there is no reason to believe others want to be treated in the same way I would like to be, or even to believe that I ought to be treated as I would like to be. For I may have a very poor idea, indeed, of what is good for me, or even what I really would like. I shall return to the Golden Rule later, in connection with a comparable thesis of Confucius. But there are a few further aspects of karma that have specifically ethical implications, and it would be worth pointing some of these out before passing to the main philosophical questions.

First of all, according to the orthodox Hindu system, there is in each of us a soul or self—an *atman*—which is the essential us. It is this *atman* that goes from life to life, and retains its identity through each karmic adventure. This inner being, whose existence is denied by Buddhism, is our highest part: indeed, as we shall see, it is one of the deepest Upanishadic teachings that the *atman* is not merely divine, but is identical with divinity. So each of us in his essential being is one with god and one with one another. Surely this could form a basis for respect and for fraternity, though it is characteristic of Hindu thought that things are not viewed solely from an anthropomorphic viewpoint, but are projected past the line that divides humans from the rest of the universe, to that point where the entire universe is permeated with the same soul-stuff that each of us bears within. And so, the Hindu is likely to feel at one with the entire universe without necessarily feeling at one with any special portion of the universe, viz., that portion consisting of other humans. Respect for life as a whole is consistent with a not especially edifying attitude towards one's fellowmen, who, for all that they may be one essentially, nevertheless remain lodged at different stations on the surfaces of the world. That they should be where they are is, as *karma* teaches, very much a matter of just desert: they are there because they deserve to be there. Our *karma* has brought each of us to whatever pass we are at. Indians tend to invoke *karma*, and hence their past wickedness, to justify the evils that befall them, much as Christians invoke their sins. As each man gets what he deserves, there seems to be no special reason to help one another. Men have only themselves to blame for what they are. Had they been better, they would be better off now. It is up to them to try for a better life next time. Present felicity, likewise, is the mark of having done well before. With a row of lifetimes in which to improve one's karmic station stretching endlessly before one, there seems very little urgency in doing very much in this brief moment. One might just as well put up with the fall of circumstance. To be sure, there is something preferable here to the Christian theory that this life is a trying place in which we win or lose momentously and forever, subject always and only to undeserved bestowal of grace. But with neither attitude is there really much room for correction of earthly conditions. One is to be charitable, but for one's own sake, in order to assure a better personal disposition—an attitude that can lead to ritualization of charity and an externalization of behavior. But beyond that, charity is not the best moral basis for social reform, which in the Indian system must seem pointless in view of the "real" problems, to which Indians tend to apply radical solutions, as we shall see.

Again, despite the fundamental oneness of people with the universe at large, neighbors and friends incidentally included, the soul is a lonely wanderer in eternity. In the end, everyone is on his own, each charged with the task of improving his *karma*. Of course, Indians are human. They know friendship and love. Men took steps to see that they would have the same wives and the same children in a next lifetime, even the same kingdom or business. But basically they believed that the person that one knows as oneself is not really him, that the body and the individuals who are related to the body are not really part of one's essential life, which is the life of the soul. Since ethics consists of rules for conduct with others, guides to right behavior, it follows that one is not essentially an ethical being: ethics belongs to the world in which one is momentarily lodged: it does not penetrate to the soul. As we shall see, the innerness that plays so important a role in the ascription of responsibilities, viz, intentions and motives, did not play a comparable role in Indian life. The conduct of life is essentially externalized, a matter of external conformity to rules; and one's sole motive for conforming to them is to derive karmic benefits. Each of us must find his way, and though it is a plight we have in common, essentially there is nothing we can do for one another.

Finally, and this perhaps gets beyond questions of ethics as such, there remains the interesting metaphysical question of what we really are. Since I am separate from the body that houses me, and indeed cannot be identified with any one of the myriad bodies I have possessed and will possess, I cannot but have an extremely abstract picture of what I really am. The self is "not this, not that," to use the negative characterization the sages offered in answer to the question "What is *Brahma* really?" *Brahma* is an impersonal deity, just as we are very impersonal persons—which is to be expected, given the general identity between *Brahma* and the *atman*. I mention these matters because they contrast with the lively preoccupation with the personality, even unto, and almost certainly logically correlative with the belief in bodily resurrection found in the Christian West. To a Westerner, there is a curious absence of personality in Indian art and literature. The psychological probe, the revelation of character, which is one aspect of the glory of Western art, are altogether lacking in India, where we have bland facades and abstract individuals. I do not offer this as a criticism, but as a fact. I shall probe it somewhat later, in discussing the *Bhagavad Gita*, in connection with a thesis I have to offer. Our close identification of ourselves with our bodies is related to our belief that we live but one lifetime in this world, that "after the first death, there is no other," as the Welsh poet Dylan Thomas wrote. As the possibilities of lifetime after endless lifetime decrease, the value and irreplaceability and uniqueness of this lifetime increases. My welfare cannot be separated from the welfare of my (only) body, any more than *I* can be separated from my body. I can afford to be careless in proportion to the looseness of attachment believed to hold between my body and myself. In the Indian scheme, salvation consists in a final dissolution of self from body, or better, from the chain of bodily existences that is my karmic history. Salvation, in Indian terms, cannot be appreciated save against the background of *karma*. I shall turn later to a consideration of *moksha*, but for the moment I would like to concentrate on spelling out some of what impress me as the logical consequences of the beliefs in *karma*.

It is a striking fact that *karma* is almost never defended or attacked in Indian philosophy. It is taken for granted. One of the fundamental presuppositions of Indian reflection, *karma* is accepted as a fact of nature, like the ebb and flow of tides or the wheeling of the planets, except that it would be difficult to find a natural fact that plays so profound a presuppositional role. Perhaps the belief in the regularity of nature in Western science would be a functional analogue, in the sense that it is difficult to formulate conditions under which we would give it up even if we could give it up, since it is exactly this belief that defines the conditions under which beliefs are given up in science. To give it up, though it be factual, would be like giving science up, and there is no scientific way of doing that. Like the concept of the uniformity of nature, the theory of *karma* becomes so intimately co-implicated with a wide class of practices that one could not seriously question it without also, and by the same criterion, questioning a set of practices that are perhaps co-extensive with the way of life that has evolved in India over millennia.

The Indians have made no arguments to speak of that "prove" the existence of *karma* and certainly no efforts to explain the mechanisms whereby it works. Occasionally it is suggested that people know certain things when they enter life that they could not have learned unless in a previous existence: and this may then require something like *karma* in order that it be explained. Plato used such an argument in the *Meno*, where an uneducated slave boy produced a geometrical proof, which Socrates slyly coaxed out of him. Plato, in explaining how the boy could have such knowledge, attempted to establish a doctrine of transmigration and of knowledge as "recollection." Of course the slave boy's intelligence enabled him, as it does us, to learn as he went along: moreover, he was given enough cues by Socrates to arrive at the correct answer. There remains the alternative theory of innate knowledge, but if this is ruled out, we are left only with evidence that a soul has migrated, and none of the retributive aspects of *karma*. The ordinary man in India would explain the fact that a man was hostile to him, assuming no other explanation were possible, as the result of his having harmed the other in an earlier karmic episode, but such an explanation can hardly be treated seriously as evidence. In the end, I suppose, one must accept *karma* or reject it on the basis of revelation, which is hard for us who do not accept the Veda as revelation. But even in India, there were some, the Buddhists, who accepted *karma*, but rejected any revelation whatever, and most emphatically rejected the vedic corpus as revealed.

There was one philosophical school in India that rejected *karma*. Needless to say, it was a heterodox school. This was *Carvaka*, or Materialism, which flourished and died very early indeed in the history of Indian philosophy. There is something almost shockingly modern in Carvaka theory and argument, and its general attack upon vedic teaching and the elaborate metaphysics woven upon the orthodox frame, remind one, details apart, of the radical positivism of our own century. The chief theory of Carvaka is an empiricist criterion of existence: nothing exists except what can be known to exist on the basis of sense experience. But the senses reveal only the existence of material objects; so only material objects exist. Since by definition, the soul is nonmaterial, the soul does not exist. Even assuming this argument were correct, it would not invalidate the doctrine of *karma* since *karma* does not presuppose the existence of soul: it is only in the orthodox system that the notion of the soul is superadded to *karma*. Buddhism, after all, found it possible to retain *karma* without the soul.

Carvaka met the obvious objections to its negative thesis by advancing the extremely bold theory that matter is intelligent, and that there is no need, therefore, to formulate nonmaterialistic theories to explain intelligent behavior. Such a theory was elaborated by Spinoza and, in a way, by Descartes, who remained as did Spinoza, nonmaterialistic. Their methodological procedure, however, was to explain as much as possible in terms of material processes alone; and it is quite remarkable how far one can go before one need appeal to any metaphysically fundamental different sort of principle. The need, perhaps, never arises.

The Carvakans have a number of linguistic arguments which are both ingenious and naive. Their argument is that, surely, such sentences as "I am fat" or "I am lean" refer to the speaker and predicate fatness and leanness of him respectively. So, since I am myself, I am a body because only bodies may sensibly be regarded as fat or lean. Since I am my body, when my body dies, I die. And death is the only release from the world. If release is bliss, and death the only release, then death must be the bliss referred to in sacred writing. Since death, while the end, cannot be the goal of life, the doctrine of *moksha* must be rejected. This life is the only life. So, as they put it, "Let a man feed on ghee though he runs in debt; when once the body becomes ashes, how can it ever return again?"

So, for Carvaka, the only end of life is *kama*, pleasure, and anything else is justified only so far as it produces *kama*. So extreme hedonistic consequences were drawn from the alleged refutation of *karma* as Professor Sharma sums them up in his *Ethical Philosophies of India:*

The enjoyment of heaven lies in eating delicious food, keeping company of young women, using fine clothes, perfumes, garlands, sandal paste, etc. The pain of hell lies in the troubles that arise from enemies, weapons, diseases. . . . Chastity and other such ordinances are laid down by clever weaklings.

If the chief reason for moral behavior is karmic amelioration, then with the dissipation of the karmic belief goes the chief reason for being moral. So with *dharma* ruled out, *kama* alone is left, and *artha* only so far as it subserves the pursuit of pleasure or does not interfere with it, as the advice to eat ghee though you run into debt suggests.

There is little to say regarding the unvarnished hedonism of Carvaka. What men like best, Aristotle remarked, is delicate food and sexual intercourse, and we may suppose that our natural drives are here. Less specifically, it is a respectable moral position that an action, or at least a principle of action is right (justified or, at least, justifiable) if it produces pleasure; and that of two acts or principles of action, the one that produces the preponderance of pleasure is morally preferable. We cannot afford to enter upon the questions to which hedonism and utilitarianism give rise, but a few words may be said regarding the abruptness of Carvaka's conclusions. They remind us, in a way, of Dostoyevsky's cry that if God is dead, every thing is permitted: if *moksha* is pointless, then anything goes. Rather, if God is dead, nothing is permitted, for God would be conceived of as He who permits and forbids, and with the death of God there falls a whole class of reasons for doing and not doing certain things: a whole class of moral beliefs loses its application. Does this mean that a man may run wild, may kill and rape or, more genially, may drink and make merry with impunity, to the neglect of all else? Or sicken himself, if he wishes, on ghee? The answer is no. The mere withdrawal of a class of justifications does not constitute a justification in its

own right. With the death of God goes only a class of reasons
for not behaving in certain ways. More likely what we would
find is that the basis for our moral beliefs would remain unal-
tered, indifferent as to whether God were alive or dead. The
surprising thing is how little difference his being alive or dead
makes to moral life.

And so with Carvaka. The repudiation of *karma* does not license license, except insofar as it seemed that the sole reason
for not indulging in license must be the deleterious consequences it had for *karma*. In that case, one may sink with impunity into abandon and delectation. And here we must think
of the context in which the Carvakans propounded their
worldly philosophy. The appetite for release in India has always been overwhelming, and asceticism has often suggested
itself as a technique for attaining it. If there is extremism in
India, it is that of austerity and worse, since preoccupation
with *moksha* more or less swamped concern over the other
aims of life. We shall see the Buddha himself combatting this
predisposition with his Middle Way. The Carvakans must be
seen as weighting *kama* with a zealousness that can only be explained with reference to the immense moral gravitation ex-
erted by its opposite. And, finally, Carvaka underscored the
extreme selfishness, the extreme self-preoccupation, of the
schools it opposed.

In any event, Carvaka did not endure. Like most philosophical positions, it enjoyed a polemical longevity, viz., it remained
always as something to refute. The common refutation of Carvaka has been merely a repetition of what it believed in,
namely materialism. So the doctrine of *karma* has had no critics to speak of in the subsequent tradition.

3

Brahma, BOREDOM,

AND RELEASE

In Voltaire's *Candide* the old female servant of Cunégonde recites for her mistress' edification a horrendous catalogue of disasters which compose the history of her life. In the end, she confesses, "Je voulus cent fois me tuer, mais j'aimais encore la vie." And this "faiblesse ridicule est peut-être un de nos penchants les plus funestes: car y a t-il rien de plus sot que de vouloir porter continuellement un fardeau qu'on veut toujours jeter par terre?" Suicide, which is commonly regarded a radical solution to our individual sorrows, a "back door, which is always open," as Epictetus describes it, can serve as a dubious comfort, though the servant acknowledges that she has known "un nombre prodigieux de personnes qui avait leur existence en exécration; mais je n'en ai vu que douze qui aient mis voluntairement fin à leur misère." It is at any rate not an avenue of escape for the Indian, or at least not the final sort of escape it seems to be to us. Whatever are the generic sorrows of life, the Indian must face them again and again, dying death after death. It is against this apparently ghastly prospect of endless deaths that the single-death theory takes on a measure of comprehensibility: if our curse is to have to live over and over, then it might indeed seem blessed to have to die but once. Whatever the case, the prospect of repeated mortalities caused a nagging pessimism in the Indian mind, and this is one of the features we must now take especially into account. After all, for one in whom the pulse of life is strong, the prospect of repeated lives could

hardly be dismal. And if the certitude of death does not cor-
rupt, but perhaps even intensifies the pleasures of life, why
should repeated deaths be any more dismal than just dying
once? In a way, one would think that the prospect of repeated
deaths would blunt the sting. Death cannot mean, as it does
for us, the flat obliteration of sense and consciousness and the
loss of the world. So it cannot hold the terror of nothingness.
It must be more like a final sleep from which we waken into
another life: and why should this be thought so grim? To be
sure, it means we must die again. But the concept of death has
been so altered that it cannot any longer mean what it would
to us. One may wake into a worse life, or it might be a better
one; and if one takes *karma* seriously, one can virtually assure
a better life. So why should repeated deaths be so horrifying?

Nietzsche believed that there is an eternal return in events,
the same things happening over and over again without any
internal differences. So I shall, as I have an endless number of
times, write my thoughts on India; and the reader will read
them endlessly—the same reader with the same thoughts
over and over again, forever. Of course, if we lived each of
these lives in innocence of the fact that it was a repeat, men
would bear each life the same way each time: they would not
know they were replicating a pattern that had been and will
be timelessly exemplified. Nietzsche experimented with the
idea of introducing the concept of our having *knowledge* of
eternal recurrence. What effect would it have? It could, of
course, change nothing. Would it be crushingly demoralizing,
however, to realize each of us is condemned to repeat the moments of our lives with no alteration and no exit? Nietzsche
thought it might be liberating. For one thing, it provided an
alternative to the vision of a last judgment and perpetual punishment. But perpetuity of any sort is difficult to accept, and I
can see the vision of eternal recurrence as singularly nauseating. Imagine having endless times to go through what we all
have gone through once, the mastering of our bodies: learning

to walk erect, learning to control our bowels, and going through all the same stages of emotional awakening again and again with all of its embarrassments, all the torments. A child would be innocent of the fact that he was doing it for the thousandth time, and he would apply the same earnestness of endeavor. But we are speaking of our knowledge that we would have to go through it again, even with some variety, —and there cannot be much, since in an infinitude of lifetimes, differences must become slight indeed. I think the knowledge would be shattering. The mere tedium of it all could not be borne. And it is this cosmic boredom, I believe, that underlies the Indian despair with life.

Seeing life as a unique episode lends a poignancy to the fleetingness of things. Individuals and moments are precious through their unreturningness. This fragility and once-for-all-time quality is a feature of the Japanese outlook—a fact that ought to alert us against making any assumptions regarding the uniformity of the Asian mind. Japanese art, in spirit, is like that of the rococo painter Watteau: a celebration of the momentary, a melancholy exaltation of what will not come again. The Japanese found in this fleeting aspect of things the chief aesthetic pleasures of life: immortality would mean a vanishing through irrelevancy of the "pity of things," to use their expression. The point of living would disappear if there were not this poignancy, they felt. Although both the Japanese and Indians were an aesthetically supercharged people, the contrast between their views of life is stark. Granting that one may get a better life, and a better one still, granting that one may rise to the estate of a king or a god and achieve intense *kama* in the pleasure gardens of Indra, still, there is a grinding monotony from episode to episode. And the question of whether there is not some way or some means whereby we might once and for all get off the senseless wheel of existence presents itself with an urgency with which it is difficult for us to sympathize. Senselessness, I think, is the chief assessment we must place upon the kind of repetition envisaged. The meaning of an episode is radically modified when the episode is repeated exactly. When a man repeats a sentence over and over again, the sentence cannot have the same meaning as it would have had if spoken only once; and things can have no meaning if they must be done again and again. This is the point at which *moksha* enters. It is relative to the meaninglessness of existence that release must be appreciated, and specifically this means release from *karma*. The immediate problem is to find out what sort of life we would have to live in order not to pay a karmic price.

One's *karma* is determined by the proportion of good and evil actions performed during life. Release from *karma*, in effect, would be release from good-and-evil, and actions that lift one above this must themselves be neither good nor evil. *Moksha* is not annihilation: it involves transport to another sort of existence. This, again, would mean being beyond good and evil. It is thus that we must understand the somewhat puzzling declarations sometimes made by Hindus that they do not recognize good and evil. They do not recognize it as a distinction that has application everywhere. It belongs to the *karma* world, to the world of trivargic actions, and, as we shall later see, to a world that is not finally real. Liberation means, inter alia, liberation from good and evil. For the individual in pursuit of *moksha*, the distinction within the world must be regarded as less important than the distinctions between the world as a whole and some higher, extraworldly station. Relative to this distinction, the distinctions within the world are not genuine distinctions at all, or at least are negligible ones. The world must be seen as all of a piece, with good no better than evil, from this vantage point. Good and evil are important only to one within the world, caught in the karmic circle. But to break out of this circle is to leave good and evil behind. To move towards release, then, is, to make a fatal half turn away from the world as such.

By common consent in India, *moksha* is the highest goal in life. It is, however, not a goal like the others. The other goals may be simultaneously pursued, but *moksha* cannot be pursued simultaneously with any of the other ends of life. It cannot coherently be pursued that way, for with one hand we would be accumulating the karmic consequences that we are seeking to cast away with the other hand. So *moksha* contrasts with and is opposed to the other three goals. It belongs in a different moral space altogether. The other goals depend upon a differentiated world. But *moksha* intends a state of undifferentiatedness:

> *Moksha as the highest goal inspires us to bury all physical and social differences, because the state of liberation can never be regarded as free from all pains and physical obstacles unless the attainment of moksha makes a person rise above the contradictions and antinomies of pleasure and pain, heat and cold, joy and fear, etc. These differences, though practical, must be resolved at the moksha level which is the level . . . free from all the* Uphadis, *or conditions that are responsible for differentiated experiences in the spatiotemporal world.*

This leveling off of distinctions is facilitated precisely by that state of monotony the karmic teaching encourages, if I have analyzed the matter correctly. For *karma* teaches us there is infinite repetition of existences, and so it serves to flatten out all distinctions within and between existences, one coming out much like another. *Karma* is then a powerful solvent of distinctions, generating the state of boredom that I have ascribed to the Hindu outlook. It is not the boredom of a child who does not know what to do on a dull afternoon. For from that boredom there is hope for diversion and relief. Rather, it is the boredom of one who has lived too long and seen too much, who knows that the future will bring only more of the same.

This is a metaphysical boredom, known by one who has seen the valleys and peaks of life and for whom the world goes stale. The energetic striver, intent upon improving his *karma*, is like the child who hopes for something better to come. The jaded personage to whom I refer knows that there is nothing better to be expected, that better and worse are faces of the same tedious coin. Boredom of this sort goes with the sense of the meaninglessness of things, the mad repetition of life after life. To have reached this state of mind is to see the world as a whole. It is the negative moment of *moksha*. *Moksha* is possible only when one is weary of the world. Only when *kama*, *artha*, and *dharma* have no hold is a man ready for release. To overcome distinctions is already to hold the world at a certain distance, is no longer, in effect, wholly to be in it.

The proliferation of distinctions always tends to decrease the differences between the elements distinguished. Black and white are absolute, uncompromising, and stark, but as the number of distinctions approaches infinity, as we might say in mathematical parody, the degree of difference between any near pair of elements approaches zero. There is an overwhelming propensity in Indian expression toward a prodigality of distinctions. The facades of temples are so extravagantly massed with gods, beasts, plants, and lovers that the play of dark and light, of shadow and surface, cancel one another out, the entirety dissolving into a great agglutinated and indiscernible mass. Things are clear at each point but shapeless as a whole. The surface profusion, the absence of focus, the absence even of pattern—for pattern involves abstractions, reductions, and orderings, there being patterns *in* life without life itself being patterned—may be said, for what it is worth, to reflect the complexities of Indian social and caste order. This verges on a surface that cannot be managed. Or it cannot be managed in its complexity. But the very complexity tends, through its multiplexity, to collapse into a singleness that a more sharply distinguished surface would reject. There is a respect in which complexity and simplicity are correlative in Indian sensibility, and one of our problems is to locate this sense.

Consider, for example, the individual. In one sense, the individual is complex. This can be seen if we attempt to fuse into one all the end-to-end bodily appearances. I cannot be said to have the properties belonging to me in any one of my phases, for then it would not be me who has the properties of the other phases. If we substract all of these properties, what is left over has to be the same in each phase, but distinct from the properties it possesses in each phase. So, in a way, there is no exact manner of describing me. The god Vishnu once was a dragon, then the god-king Rama, then the god Krishna, and even later the historical Buddha, not a god any longer, since Buddha was but a man. So Vishnu is all and none of these. He is complex and simple at once, as we all are simple and complex at once.

The *Katha Upanishad* says: "Whoever sees manyness in the world sees death and meets death." To avoid death, which is to avoid *karma*, one must see not manyness but oneness. The overcoming of distinction is an intellectual passion in traditional Indian thought and a means to salvation. It is the knowledge of the oneness beneath surfaces that is the supposedly saving insight. In one of the Upanishads, the woman Gargya asks how many gods there are. With each answer, she repeats the question, and gets a lower number. Finally there are three and a half gods, and when she asks once more, she is told not to ask so many questions, or her head will fall off. The impulse is characteristic. And the technique for gratifying the impulse is by means of establishing identities. The *Brihidaranyika Upanishad* begins with a series of identities between the elements of the horse sacrifice and the cosmos: the dawn is the head of the horse, etc. To perform the sacrifice is accordingly to recreate the world. And not in effigy nor in ritual, but in fact, given the identifications. Fire does not represent the fire god. It is the fire god. So if I control the fire, I control the fire god. If I con-

trol the fire, I am the fire, and so the fire god. This is characteristic Vedic thinking, and the identificatory process continues into the Upanishads. The famous Upanishadic utterance is
the *Tat Twam Asi*—"Thou art that"—in which a young
man is instructed in a sequence of identifications. Any basis for
an identification is seized, and when an identification is
achieved, a distinction collapses. Apparently this can go on
until everything is identified with everything, and all distinctions vanish. Thus since Krishna is Buddha, the distinction between them collapses. What then is left? Just the self, which is
Krishna-Buddha, and neither of them. How many selves are
there? Well, when we consider a pair of individuals, a and b,
and assume that a has had two phases and b two phases; and
that a is neither of his phases and b is neither of his, then what
remains to distinguish a from b? The answer is nothing, and
the formula appears to be that if nothing distinguishes a from
b, then a and b are one. So there can be at most one self, since
the formula is always applicable until the last distinction has
been washed away. When I have overcome the world, I have
overcome death; and when I have overcome death, I have
overcome *karma*. So the transcendance of *karma* is the transcendance of multiplicity, and this demands an intellectual
achievement of the sort to which the Upanishads are the
guide. The release that is *moksha* is release from multiplicity.
And the mechanism is the identification of differences.

I have suggested that the sense of sameness is prepared for in
the feeling of boredom that comes with the prospect of infinite
repetition. The intellectual insight, if we may call it that, is
that differences collapse into identity, if we could but see past
the tedious surface. Distinctions, which seem to articulate the
surface of existence, are unreal.

Let us pause for a moment to make some comparison with
our own Western traditions. The famous speculation with
which philosophy is said to have begun—the thesis that all is
water, which was pronounced by the Greek philosopher

Thales—suggests that the distinction between fluid, gas, and solid, is not a fundamental distinction, but rather that each state is a stage of the single, same stuff. One could, in fact, say that this stuff, of which these are stages, is itself neither fluid, nor solid, nor gaseous: and this would have been at once a more audacious and a more scientific way of thinking. The history of scientific advance is full of such sweeping reductions: the atomic theory of matter, the kinetic theory of heat, the quantum theory of mechanics, are all cases where the distinctions that appear on the surface of the world are found, or claimed, not to belong to the fundamental stuff of which the world is composed. The atoms are colorless, that is, achromatic, and athermal. And indeed this must be the case. We explain the variations in temperature of a body of gas in terms of the deviations from the average velocity of the molecules that compose it. But if heat is caused by the energy of molecules in random motion, heat is not predicable of molecules, taken one at a time. I say this must be the case if we are to explain the existence of heat. If we said that heat in a body of gas were due to the sum of the heats of the molecules that compose it, we would have explained the concept of heat-of-a-body, but not the concept of heat as such: for this we must use concepts in which the notion of heat does not appear. You cannot explain heat by referring to heat! So, it follows that whatever you use to explain a phenomenon cannot have the properties of the phenomenon explained, or there would be no explanation. It follows, then, that the way in which scientists conceive the world has to be different from the way in which others conceive of it, but it does not follow that their world is the "real" one, as philosophers in the seventeenth century surmised, but rather that the world as they conceive of it has to be different if they are to base explanations of our world upon it. So, when the scientist refers to a world beneath the world, to which the distinctions pertaining to the former fail to apply, he is not necessarily denying that those distinctions are real:

rather, he is concerned to explain them. In this way, one hopefully returns to the surface with a better understanding of the distinctions variegating it. One overcomes distinctions only in order to account for them. Science is not magic.

In India things took a different turn. The surface is not to be explained but eliminated; and, we are not required to account for distinctions—we cannot, since they are not real —but at best, to understand why there seem to be distinctions. Since they do not exist, but only seem to, it is natural to employ the idiom of illusion in discussing the surfaces of the world. And since the problem with illusions is not to account for their content but why we have them, the world in which distinctions occur lies outside the compass of meaningful discussion. When we see this world as illusion, it has no hold upon us any longer, or should have none. We have seen through it. And, again, this is release. The fundamental release from the world comes with the insight that there is no world to be released from. Liberation from *karma* is the profound recognition that there is no *karma*. It is like waking from a dream.

So although there is a precocious turn away from surfaces in India, nothing remotely like our concept of science ever arose. The sages of Upanishadic literature were interested in escape rather than understanding, their view being that the world they sought to escape had not been there to be understood to begin with.

Passage to India, E. M. Forster's masterwork, contains some vivid representations of these peculiarities of Indian thought. The first is the shattering mystical experience undergone in the Marabar Caves by Mrs. Moore. When we first encounter Mrs. Moore, we find her genuinely, if rather conventionally, pious and personally rather saintly. She sees persons as persons, unlike her British compatriots, who cannot see Indians as other than Indians. The Marabar Caves, to which she goes as a chaperone and guest rather than as a pilgrim, are great bubbles of emptiness. One is much as another, and to see one is to see them all, though "see" is perhaps the wrong word, given their great darkness. The image of the caves is striking, they are vacuities separated from the surrounding air by dirt. But for the intervening dirt, there would be no caves, and no darkness. To destroy the wall separating nothing from nothing would be to wipe out a distinction between emptiness and emptiness: which is no distinction at all. At one point in the *Chandogya*, a father orders his son to cut open a seed and to say what is in it. There is, of course, nothing, but from this nothing would have sprung forth forests of mustard plants; and the father says to his son "Thou art that." The caves have a peculiar echo. It is in its own terms an undistinguished "bou-oum," interestingly reminiscent of the sacred syllable *Om*. *Om* is the answer to all questions as the "bou-oum" is the undifferentiated echo given back by any noise. One may belch in the void, and it comes back "bou-oum." Or one may shout divine poetry, and it will be no different. In the dark fetid caves, with their absurd echoes, all distinctions are smudged, nothing makes a difference, everything is: bou-oum.

It is a moment of truth for Mrs. Moore, but not the truth she expected. In fact, the truth she expected would be merely lost and undiscernible in the maddening echo. The Western mystical literature is a literature of ecstasy and embrace. Santa Teresa is alone on her cloud, individuated at the moment of unity, when she is pierced by a golden arrow. Mrs. Moore's experience is, instead, an Oriental blur and a profound spiritual dislocation rather than a fulfillment. But, as Forster remarks in an aside that is almost unendurably sardonic; "Wait until you have had one, dear reader." Mrs. Moore was never the same again. She died soon afterwards at sea, after having gone sour as a human being. It was not an uplifting experience. Merely human problems no longer much interested her. She went crotchety and irritable. She also became a god. Not in a literal way, of course, but in an Indian way: because of her testimony at a trial in which a Muslim doctor is accused of raping an English girl, her name goes round as a noise of hope. It becomes transformed into Essmis-essmor. In time the name is chanted, and offerings are made, by persons who have no idea of whom Essmiss-essmor may be. She perished and the anonymous noise that was her name joined the immense pantheon of obscure secondary gods. What she went through seems at once fundamental and pointless. The cheery messages of Christmas religiosity seem falsetto and silly by contrast. One feels that if there is truth to religion at all, it is the unavailing and nauseating sort of truth that destroys a person's humanity and mind.

The other scene in Forster's book that is especially apt is the one in which Doctor Godbole, a learned and devout Hindu, is celebrating through a dance the birth of Krishna. It is a merry holiday, like Christmas, and, not unlike Christmas, is celebrated in a messy indigestable sort of way. In the course of his dance, Godbole touches what is obviously the religious climax of his life, or, in his terms, his present life. In a kind of trance, he unites in a bond of love with a fussy, old English woman—it is Mrs. Moore, as it happens, although Doctor Godbole is no longer aware of the identity of the being between whom and himself a barrier has been mystically dissolved. He also unites with a wasp. Godbole now tries for more. Into the unity of himself, Essmiss-essmor, and the wasp, he seeks to assimilate the lump of mud upon which the wasp is poised. It is too much for him. The spell breaks. Godbole surfaces from the deep selflessness of his mystic dance relatively satisfied with his achievement. He has eradicated a few distinctions—between himself, an old woman, and a wasp. It is not much in one sense, but it is a momentous achievement in another. Relative to the vast sea of differences, it is a minor erasure. But it is something. It is a genuine overcoming. Mere friendship and common affection cannot attain to this. We realize this at the end of the book, when two friends, with the greatest will towards reconciliation, cannot dissolve what separates them. But at the climax of the book, after Godbole's dance, and at a climactic moment of the Krishna festival, the paraphernalia of celebration are thrown into a lake. A storm has come up. There is a great thunderclap, like a mallet splitting a rock. One is certain that a Marabar Cave has been at once destroyed and redeemed. There are people on the lake. Their boat capsizes. The surface of the lake is a chaos of humanity and sacred debris, and in the sodden cataclysm a husband and wife are thrown together, with the result, we are led to understand, that a sexually difficult and tepid marriage was saved. Again, it is not much. It is a minor dissolution of separateness. But as before, it is something, and perhaps as much grace as we can expect in one lifetime. From the disproportion between effort and attainment, we can appreciate the immensity of the problem and the unlikelihood of its solution. But we have no choices save to continue.

Sexual union has been the paradigm for mystical union in all religious literature. It is as close as common people come to the resolution of distinctions to which the mystic aspires. At the climax of bliss, differences between partners melt away in a paroxysm of ectasy. But climaxes are not plateaus. Glory recedes. The momentarily united couple lapse into routine apartness, and the separation is all the more painful for having been overcome. Mrs. Moore is embittered by her experience, and it is not plain that Godbole's satisfaction can last for long. If bliss is the blotting out of difference, then residual differences are obstacles to bliss; and even if we are convinced of their illusoriness, they are none the less felt as painful. It becomes a pressing question whether separateness can be held indefinitely at bay. It is in response to this question that an elaborate technology of ecstasy arises in India, to be understood as mechanisms for reducing the variety of experience's senseless flow. Deep breathing, relaxation, calisthenics, meditation, and trance, all have the effect of slowing to a standstill the passing stream of life, immobilizing and excluding it as one adopts the ascetic posture. It is very different, of course, from sexual intensity. It is, by contrast, extreme apathy. But it aims at the same result, though without the same lapse. It involves extreme control in contrast with the extreme loss of control at the peak of intimacy. Yet in the same way, more or less, it involves a loss of the world through a loss of the self. I shall characterize it in these terms.

Meditation requires concentration, or, perhaps, is concentration. One begins by concentrating upon some object, say a doorknob, or the tip of one's nose or one's navel, it not really mattering which. The thing is to hold one's attention on the object, whatever it may be, for increasing periods of time, while excluding any collateral mental or physical activity. This is extremely difficult to do. One finds one's mind— one's "vagabond mind," in Descartes' felicitous phrase— will have wandered off, which is natural given the practical energies of our intellect, which is always projecting fantasies and schemes. The purpose of the object concentrated upon is to serve as an anchor for the surging activity of the mind: one has no real sense of how wildly active the mind is until one attempts this sort of activity: it is rather like attempting to arrest a stream by driving a stake into the stream bed, which in fact merely serves to articulate eddies, formed as the stream surges on in its course. At any rate, the thing is to put the "mind-stuff at rest," as the *Yoga Sutra* describes this phase of meditation. The *Gita* has passages in which meditation is described as "fixing the thought-organ on a single object/ Restraining the activity of his mind and senses/. . . Even body, head, and neck,/ Holding motionless, (keeping himself) steady,/Gazing at the tip of his nose,/ And not looking in any direction . . ." (VI:12−13).

Let us suppose this state has been attained: one can fall into the state of cessation of mental activity for increasingly protracted periods. Holding the mind steady by means of the doorknob, we realize, is using a crutch. But in the meditative phase the rest of the world has fallen away. Now let me speak somewhat technically for a moment. There is here a mental act, which is heeding or fixing, and a certain content. The problem is to subtract the content, which is intrinsically detached of meaning anyway, leaving only the act. You may argue that this cannot be done. You cannot have the heeding when nothing is heeded, the state of heeding being logically transitive. So, in effect, to subtract the content is to substract the act as well. So far as this would be done, the result would be wholly satisfactory, however, for what would be left in that case would be the individual himself, the heeder, no longer engaged in even the mental act of concentration, and finally alone in himself. "The enjoyments that spring from outside contacts/Are nothing but sources of misery," the *Gita* says, "With self unattached to outside contacts,/When he finds happiness in the self/He . . . attains imperishable bliss" (V:21). What we have here, of course, is a state of extreme undifferentiatedness. There is no content and no act. There is only self, with nothing to modify its utter simplicity. The question remains: What sort of bliss is promised here? I cannot but feel that it is a passive bliss, a state not of affect but of absence of affect, a state in which there is no experience but the absence of experience, a state of pure and undisturbed repose. It is not pure negativity for the self continues to exist in its integrity. Since it exists and nothing happens to it, it avoids *karma*. And so avoids the feared second death. Of course, it is not final release. But it is a means to it, and it is as close to it as we may come while still tethered to the karmic world.

Like anything else, yogic discipline may be vulgarized. It has a sublime and philosophical aspect, but it has an unedifying nether side. The philosophical school of Yoga, which was one of the orthodoxies, is characterized by dualisms. In contrast with Vedanta, Yoga insists upon the reality of the world and concentrates upon means to transcend it. It developed a corollary calisthenic, the Hatha Yoga, involving a considerable degree of bodily and mental self-control. Bodily control is a means to mental control, and both are means of escape into the self. But in the process of control, the body and the mind—in Indian thought, the mind is an instrument of the body, like the senses—remains located in the world. All sorts of worldly gains and special abilities are promised as the product of control. One will be able to forecast the future, to attain incredible sexual and physical powers, to levitate, and the like. Intermediate between the two extremes of self-control and superhuman powers are the mere therapeutic advantages of yoga. It certainly confers inner peace and healthy muscle tone, if nothing else. But I should like to dwell briefly upon the shadier side, the wonder-working side of asceticism, for it is always connected with popular religio-philosophical thought, and it serves to illuminate some features of practical morality. After all, the hope of miracles forms the vulgar basis of religious belief. Moreover, we must recognize the immense prestige that attaches to the ascetic, given the structure of the Hindu scheme of values. The ascetic pursues the highest acknowledged value. He also is beyond good and evil, for he has renounced trivargic values altogether. So this puts him at once high in the moral scheme and outside the conventional moral scheme, which is worked out specifically in connection with trivargic acts.

The role of the ascetic must be one that is tempting to exploit. For one thing, the ascetic is a licensed Bohemian, relieved from ordinary responsibilities and duties. It is a tribute to the unconscious genius of the Indian social structure that it provides a place for individuals who do not fit into the usual social structure. The Bohemian is accommodated to a structure flexible enough to contain him, in contrast with other social structures, in which the religious Bohemian is a threat and regarded as such. In medieval Islam, for example, the mystics constituted, or appeared to constitute, a danger to religious authority and to the social structure as well, for they were bent

upon making direct contact with Allah, and impugned the re-
straints and conventions binding upon the more pedestrian devout. So inevitably there was a contest between adherents of
enthusiasm and discipline, between practical religion, which
was the cement of society, and personal religion which was,
perforce, antisocial. Indeed, the mystic might deliberately flout
the social order to exhibit the dependence upon a more direct
grace, and after all, does not Allah save whom He will? There
is an extraordinary work, a classic of Arabic which belongs
to world literature, the *Assemblies of Al Hariri*, in which
these contrasts are marvelously exhibited.

The dubious hero of the *Assemblies* is a reprobate and a
confidence man, Abu Zayd, gifted with the rhetorically agile
tongue so prized among the Arabs. He eked out a living by
delivering seemingly inspired speeches to the pious, who are
recalled to their commitment and profoundly, religiously
moved by them. He is always well-rewarded, and spends his
earnings in ways antithetical to the content of the speeches by
which he gains them: womanizing, drinking, and in idle enter-
tainment. His are sins compounded by hypocrisy. His foil, the
well-meaning and conventionally moral narrator of the *Assemblies*, consistently underscores the discrepancies between Abu
Zayd's words and his deeds in forty-odd episodes of duplicity.
Yet in the end Abu Zayd is saved, whether because Allah's
will is inscrutable, because Abu Zayd's genius remained an instrument of faith regardless of his behavior, or perhaps because
true piety is imprescriptible. "I knew for certain," the narrator
says, "that in our dispensation inspired ones are found." One
wonders whether the narrator had a sudden realization of his
own peril, as though his uprightness guaranteed nothing. It is a
beautiful frightening contrast, one we find over and over when
duty abrades freedom: as though Abu Zayd were the dream of
freedom of those entrapped in rectitudes. We shall encounter
another such moral *Doppelgänger* in China.

The ascetic in India does not subvert the social order that

has made a place for him. But individuals can exploit a role that brings worldly advantages, even though they are not spiritually qualified to play that role themselves. And it is here that the feats of ascetic self-control, which are spiritually only by-products of discipline, serve as emblems of an advantageous status. This avenue of nefariousness is treated as the theme of R. J. Narayan's great comic novel, *The Guide*. His picaresque hero, who scrambles in order to keep afloat on the surfaces of life and makes a precarious living as a guide, gets into trouble and seeks refuge near a village temple. He decides to act like a holy man; he lets his hair grow and eats well on the food left as sacrifices by the simple people of the community, who are pleased that a holy man has graced their locale. He is a valuable presence. However, a price must be paid. During a local drought, the erstwhile guide finds that the people expect him to fast in order to cause its end. People come to watch and admire his discipline and to derive the immense spiritual benefit that his holy presence confers. So he is forced to live the role, which he does, and in the process is transformed. Moreover, his transformation coincides with the rainfall he is credited with having brought. We are reminded of the ambiguity of the concept of a guide. Travelers know guides as scruffy marginal figures, not far removed from pimps. But Virgil is a guide, and so is Beatrice, who leads Dante to Paradise. Narayan's hero plays both roles, and his transformation from the one sort of guide to the other is a paradigm of the kind of transfiguration that *moksha* ideally intends.

Moksha, which has a profound religious meaning, is not a moral concept. It *contrasts* with moral concepts, and in pursuing *moksha*, we occupy a station beyond good and evil, and so beyond morality. In seeking to fulfill this end, one turns one's back upon the world and upon the human scene. There is something inhuman in the concept of *moksha*, as is inevitable, given that our concept of humanity is inextricably involved with matters of good and evil and of life in the world it is the task and essence of *moksha* to remove us from. The holy man is not one of us, and his presence is a disturbing one. He is a paradigm not for living better lives, but for fleeing life altogether. But it is a life impregnated by a concept without which, perhaps, *moksha* would not have the appeal it evidently has. If we are not persuaded that life is rendered senseless through repeated deaths of oneself, the need of and consequent obsession with release becomes decreasingly relevant.

4

THERAPY AND THEOLOGY

IN BUDDHIST THOUGHT

Buddhism's instant appeal is due to the seeming simplicity of its message and its resolute unconcern with questions that do not immediately bear upon the burden of its glad tidings. The Buddha himself comes on as a sympathetic personality who makes no special claims of possessing extraordinary powers and who manages to convey his teaching through transparent images and arresting parables. Buddha affects the role merely of the author, or discoverer of a genuine solution to a very considerable human problem. That problem is suffering, the cause and cure of which the Buddha claims not merely to know but to be able without superhuman difficulty to teach. The solution is universal and radical: it is addressed to suffering as such, and not to this sort of suffering or that. It is because of this that Buddhism qualifies as a religion rather than a form of therapy. It is because of this, as well, that its moral relevance is uncertain.

Neither the cause nor the cure of suffering, as Buddha understands them, are matters of revelation, except in the sense in which every new idea is a revelation; and Buddha's marvelous idea is not only that anyone with sufficient enterprise could have thought it all out, but that anyone can apply the knowledge to his own case without the aid or mediation of experts. So the Buddha appears to himself and to his immediate disciples as a doctor for the generalized ills of mankind. In contrast with the orthodox formulae for *moksha*, the Buddhist regimen is accessible to anyone at any time and is indifferent to caste standing. It requires neither mastery of an arcane doctrine—the Buddha is rather anti-intellectual regarding learning that does not directly apply to questions that he, with some justice, regards as urgent—nor elaborate programs of austerity. The understanding and enactment of the Buddhist prescription is well within the limits of common intelligence and will. The Buddha is a self-proclaimed advocate of the Middle Path, midway between the extremes of hedonism (recall the teaching of Carvaka) and asceticism. It is a path that leads to the precise end sought by hedonists, who mean to drown out pain by unremitting pleasure, and by ascetics, who mean to escape pain by sinking into a state of apathy and slipping from the opposites of pain-and-pleasure through their programs of discipline. Most important, the Buddha promises immediate release, in the respect that there is no need to work one's way through a sequence of karmic stages to some remote stage at which release is feasible. That release may come directly and to anyone is dramatically underscored in that exotic branch of Buddhist teaching, namely Zen, which, by some paradox of history, has become a household word in recent times. Zen had a great appeal for artists, who are inherently subject to the great temptation, as Yeats described it, of "creation without labor," and its popularity coincided with a theory of art according to which art is an activity rather than a product, to be judged primarily, if not exclusively, in terms of spontaneousness. This went together with a story of studied inarticulateness and anti-intellectualism. The heroes of Zen, characteristically, are not philosophers and theoreticians, but peasants and kitchen workers. But this view of the mystic potentialities of the humble man is an almost universal element of religious mythology. It is always the simple and lowly who manage to attain the revelations, while the mighty and the bright are excluded precisely through their power and intelligence. I will return to this topic later. For the moment I prefer to restrict the discussion to the standard Buddhist teachings, only certain elements of which are accentuated in Zen. As we shall see, and characteristic of Indian thought, the path to salvation is through knowledge in Buddhism, even in Zen; and though there are different ways of understanding the concept of knowledge, which accounts for the differences, the fact remains that in one guise or another, knowledge is the central concept of Buddhism.

Buddha's original teaching, which remains a common fund for all branches of Buddhist thought, is expressed in the Four Noble Truths. These are four distinct propositions, the internal mastery of which insures release from suffering. I stress internal mastery, because it is not enough merely to attain an abstract understanding of the propositions. One has to make them part of one's life. After all, they are considered as medicine. And medicine has to be taken. It does your headache no good to have aspirins in the medicine chest. This can be said generally of religious knowledge, I think. It has to be internalized, which is a main crux of disputes between believers and nonbelievers. Nonbelievers have to be convinced that they are sick!

The First Noble Truth is that suffering exists. This may be thought obvious enough, but the legend is that it was something Buddha had to discover. He was a prince, Siddhartha, extremely protected by his parents, whose motives I sympathize with, from the concept of suffering. He grew to young manhood in Kapilavastu without an awareness of the existence of suffering, passing a paradisal life in the palace and park of his indulgent father and step-mother, who provided him with a lovely wife and all his uninstructed heart could wish. One day he encountered a cripple, a child, an old man, and a corpse, and the existence of suffering came home to him with the intensity of a revelation. As he put it, "Birth is painful, old age is painful, sickness is painful, death is painful, sorrow, lamentation, dejection, and despair are painful. Contact with unpleasant things is painful, not getting one's wishes is painful."

There is much to be said for the First Noble Truth, even though it appears a commonplace. For Buddha, the "Enlightened One," did not announce it as a commonplace, but propounds it as a problem. To treat it as a problem is already to put oneself in position to think of it as something that might have a solution. So the First Noble Truth has almost the quality of a philosophical statement. It is characteristic of philosophy to find the commonplace puzzling. Everyone in a way knows the First Noble Truth, but it took a virtual act of genius to see it as the sort of truth that the Buddha did. Everyone suffers. But not everyone knows that he suffers. Suffering is a passion. To know that it is suffering is not a passion, but a piece of knowledge. What the Buddha recognized is that knowledge of the fact can be step towards its mitigation. The first, and in some ways the hardest, step for a certain sort of sick man to make is towards the knowledge that he *is* sick. Indeed, until this step is taken, in many cases at least (and especially in the case of mental sickness) no other step can be taken at all. The Buddha also recognized that it is in some measure a mitigation of suffering to know that suffering is universal. When an adolescent realizes that he is an adolescent, that his sufferings are exactly the sufferings of his kind, he has taken a step towards the mitigation of his ills. One of the Buddha's celebrated cures—he performed no miracles—was of a mother, who, mad with grief, asked him to restore her child to life: he told her he required only a mustard seed from any house where there had not been a death, and of course she could not find this. What she did find is that the condition she lamented was a universal condition and that restoring the child to life would only postpone an inevitable fact. Nothing was changed by what the Buddha did. Only, she saw the same facts in a different way and seeing them so, she was transformed.

The Second Noble Truth explains the cause of suffering as desire or craving, or thirst (*tanha*). This is perhaps the most distinctive Buddhist teaching, that suffering is the product of "the craving of the passions, the craving for existence, the craving for nonexistence." It is, however, far from an obvious truth. Certain cases of suffering are plainly due to craving, namely, those that are due to frustrated desires. Desires may be eased by satisfaction or extirpation; and one may allow that if one stopped desiring, it would amount to preventing all the suffering due to frustration. But this does not prove the general case. To accommodate this, Buddhist analysis departs rather abruptly from its original simplicity, and becomes recognizably implicated with Indian thought in general. The desire that is the critical desire becomes the desire connected with *karma:* the desire to escape death, or to escape redeath. This desire can be overcome, but only with the removal of the central facts concerning *karma.* It is, in the end, this ignorance that allows the craving to persist. Ignorance might be said to be the cause of suffering in the sense that except and until we understand the nature of craving, we are likely to persist in it. Indeed, we will persist in it. The Buddha does not deny *karma.* One of the main sources of suffering is provided by *karma,* both in itself and in the fact that in each phase we have to endure birth and death, almost certainly disease, and very likely old age. One of the things the Buddha promises is an escape from *karma.* In order to understand it, we must work out his teaching on craving, to which I turn now.

The Buddha rejected the *atman* theory of Vedic and Upanishadic thought. We are not made up of body and soul. Rather, we are made of up groups of what are called "graspings." Body, feelings, perception, mentality, and consciousness are separate sets of graspings. There is nothing that *does* the grasping. We are the aggregate of the graspings, not something, apart from them, that does the grasping. This is an interesting and startling thought. It is brilliantly argued by Nagasina in *The Questions of King Milinda,* who points out to the king that, just as a carriage is nothing, separate from wheels and shafts and the like, that might be said to *have* wheels, so we are not something separate from limbs and feelings either. We are our parts, we are not something that has those parts. Readers of Gilbert Ryle and many modern philosophical psychologists will be struck by the resemblance to their own theses, regarded as avant-garde all these centuries after Buddha.

At this point it will be useful to quote at length from a typical piece of diagnostic philosophy out of the Buddhist corpus. The following exhibits that affection for chain argumentation so congenial to the logical temper of India: and it reveals the complexities of thought that the Second Noble Truth condenses. One might compare it with the original formulation in the celebrated and profound *Sermon at Benares*, where Buddha states:

> *Now this, monks, is the noble truth of the cause of pain: the craving, which tends to rebirth, combined with pleasure and lust, finding pleasure here and there; namely, the craving for passion, the craving for existence, the craving for non-existence.*

The passage I have in mind is a response to the question of how craving might in general be cause of pain:

> *Conditioned by ignorance are the karma-formations; conditioned by the karma-formations is consciousness; conditioned by consciousness is mind-and-body; conditioned by mind-and-body are the six-sense-fields; conditioned by the six-sense-fields is impression; conditioned by impression is feeling; conditioned by feeling is craving; conditioned by craving is grasping; conditioned by grasping is becoming; conditioned by becoming is birth; conditioned by birth there come into being aging and dying, grief, sorrow, suffering, lamentation and despair. Thus is the origin of the whole mass of suffering.*

It is clear that craving has been relegated to a transitional state here, and that it is really ignorance, that once removed leads to the removal of the rest: by stopping it we stop the rest: "Thus is the stopping of the whole mass of suffering." This is, I think, a dark teaching, and we might pause to reflect on what perhaps plays a crucial intermediate role in the chain and its removal, namely consciousness.

What I am conscious of is what affects me. To be conscious of anything is to be conscious of myself as related to that thing, whatever it may be. Consciousness separates the world, as it were, into two distinct parts: what is me and what is not me, but rather affects me. In particular, I am conscious of part of the world as my body. The body would be there, whether or not I were conscious of it, but it would be just a material object, a thing amongst things, until marked out by consciousness as mine. "Mineness" does not belong to the order of things: it comes into existence only when there is consciousness. If I were not conscious of the difference between mine and not-mine, there really would not be a difference. It is a difference that consciousness creates. This is an extremely searching observation, and it underlies and explains the seemingly false or senseless proposition advanced by the Buddha, namely that consciousness is the cause of body. He must mean it in the sense of "my" body. Physically, if I did not have the kind of body I have, I would not be conscious, but philosophically, I would not have "my" body if I were not conscious. So consciousness is the cause of (my) body. Built into consciousness, therefore, is an element of selfness, and of "my" sake, for which I do certain things. Each of us acts for his own sake in order, to put it in modern terms, to maximize his own utility. Insofar as this is true, action is a presupposition of consciousness. Ignorance causes action, however. For in falsely believing that I am something that has needs, which is a separate entity, I act. Ignorance, i.e., false belief, is the cause of action, which is then the cause of consciousness. What we have is a chain of causes. There is no desire without sensation, for I desire what I perceive. But there is no sensation without consciousness, for sensation demands a distance between me and something— an object of sensation—and this distance is caused by consciousness, as we saw. So consciousness is the cause of sensation and of desire, for desire is of what I have not, and I could not acknowledge having and not having were it not for the emptiness in the center of things, which consciousness explains. Desire, Buddha claims, leads me to cling to life. Life is birth and death, rebirth and redeath. By definition, these are items of suffering. So, through a chain of causes originating in ignorance and mediated through consciousness, we are led to cling to life and to suffering. This is a complex and rather dubious analysis. I am not certain I have reconstructed it correctly, but it is the most I can make of the chain of causes typically referred to in connection with the Second Noble Truth. It is rather much to expect that a simple peasant should understand this, and it is fortunate that the Buddha had the great gift that religious teachers always have, which is to express fundamental theses in parable. But we must remember that the Buddha spent eight years in meditation under the celebrated Bo tree, and it is unlikely that a man of his intelligence would need to spend that much time merely to turn over banalities. At any rate, we are obliged to deal philosophically with the theory within the limits of our present format. Surely the most questionable part of the Buddha's analysis is that it is craving that holds us to life, and that so long as we do hold to life, we shall be subject to *karma*. And so one must accept *karma* for the Second Noble Truth to have the force that those paradigms, in which suffering really is due to (unrequited) desires, would suggest.

Indeed, in order to accept this truth at all, one is obliged to accept a considerable amount of metaphysical equipment. In view of this, it appears rather disingenuous of the Buddha to pretend an unconcern with metaphysical questions, as "not leading to enlightenment." However, if we look at the actual discussions in which this view is advanced, we shall note that only certain metaphysical questions are ruled out, questions concerning the eternity and the extension of the universe, whether matter is intelligent, and whether those who are enlightened enter paradise. He deemed these questions irrelevant to the fundamental task of attaining peace, and perhaps it was his view that those who are seriously interested in solving the problem of suffering have enough to do without dispersing their limited energies in merely satisfying abstract curiosity. There is an urgency in the Buddha's message: as he put it, when a man is removing a poisoned arrow, you do not insist on knowing who made the arrow and who shot it first: the essential thing is to get it out.

The Third Noble Truth is the assurance that suffering can be completely cured, a formulation that once more underscores the fundamental Buddhist attitude that suffering is a disease. The cure is up to us. We must stop craving. This truth, as the other Noble Truths, is set forth with homely paradigms but has a complex metaphysical foundation. The paradigms run through the entire Buddhist literature. The prince who longs for his lovely wife is given women so much more ravishing than she that in his eyes his wife appears to be a crone. He does not now regret having left her, and it is pointed out to him that when, as he will have to, he must leave these beauties as well he will repeat a sorrow that in retrospect he will find laughable and pathetic. He must learn to put a distance between himself and women. Another prince nags at a lovely nun, raves over her beautiful eyes, and is handed the eyes, which abruptly extinguishes his desire. But bit by bit the metaphysical teaching becomes dominant: the world that we treasure is nothing but an illusion. There is no self to desire and no world to be desired. When we see through to the nothingness of things, we cannot take seriously the desires we had when the world was thought to have a solidity it really lacks. These are Hindu teachings, argued subtly and fanatically in abstruse works such as the philosophical poem *Mudyamaka Carakas*, of Nagarjuna, founder of the Madhyamika school of Buddhism. The simple mind could hardly penetrate the surface of these teachings, any more than the devout serf could have penetrated the philosophy of Saint Thomas; but there are levels and levels of teaching. Buddhism runs the conventional intellectual gamut of most religions, though it has a consistency between its most abstract and its most picturesque expressions that few religions have.

The Fourth, and final, Noble Truth announces the way to peace. This is the Eightfold Path: right views, right intention, right speech, right action, right livelihood, right effort, right mindness, and right concentration. The Eightfold Path raises a point which, while perhaps neither implied nor presupposed by Buddhist teaching as such, is a crucial institutional fact connected with the spread of Buddhism. It is that the Eightfold Path is a regimen involving complete dedication. It is not something one can do casually and hope to get the aimed for results. You really have to enter into the cure, or you are certain to persist in suffering. So it is not surprising that a group of followers should have detached themselves from their daily world and formed themselves into a specifically monastic body. In the early sermons and homilies, it is monks who are addressed by the Buddha. Monks are individuals upon whom the grip of the world is already looser than it is upon most of us. It is, to be sure, a cheerful order. The Middle Way dispenses with great austerities. Moreover, it is open to anyone, whatever one's sex or caste. The monk leaves the world, dons the yellow robe, and embarks upon the Eightfold Path to release. But for just these reasons, Buddhism does not work out a true lay morality, as Max Weber has pointed out. The layman, who is usually a householder and a businessman concerned with the prosperity of his family and his enterprises, cannot have internalized the Buddhist teaching. He is too attached to the "red dust" as the Chinese Buddhists called the world, and so cannot put into practice what he might accept in principle. When the hold of the world is strong, it is hard to put Buddhism into practice: and if you cannot practice it, you are not ready for it. If you are not ready for it, what meaning can it really have for you? The monk, we might say, has an existential knowledge of Buddhism. But we have argued that there is no genuine alternative. So to the layman, Buddhism has little to offer beyond the conventional homilies.

It is against this polarization of Buddhist adherents into an active monastic order and an inert laity that we must appreciate the genius of *Mahayana* Buddhism, the so-called Greater Vehicle. *Theravada* Buddhism, the Doctrine of the Elders, or the Lesser Vehicle, as it was contemptuously designated by Mahayanists is what we have been discussing thus far. Its hero is the *arhat*, a monk who has followed the dying injunction of the Buddha to work out one's salvation diligently. He has followed the Eightfold Path and is unattached, on the threshold of Nirvana or peace. He makes his departure solo. The order of monks is an order of potential *arhats*, individuals who look each to his own redemption. But, in fact, it may be argued that the concept of "salvation" is inconsistent with Buddhist teaching. It is so because the distinction between "mine" and "not-mine" is not a genuine or ultimate one. It is exactly this "mine" which must be overcome and transcended through an analysis of the nature of the self. Selflessness is a metaphysical thesis of Buddhism, not an ethical teaching, though it is transformed into something like that in Mahayana. Salvation in Mahayana comes when "my" and "it" and "you" are washed away as distinctions. None are saved until all are saved, though in effect this means that the delusive selfness of each must be revealed as false. At any rate, the *arhat*'s concern with his own salvation is necessarily frustrated. It is so because he persists in thinking of himself as a self, and in the end he is as selfish and as attached and grasping as any. Perhaps more so. In the *Lotus Sutra*, one of the great texts of Mahayana, the *arhats*—those

who heeded Buddha's words to be 'lamps unto yourselves'—
are dealt with sternly.

In Mahayana, the *arhat* gives way to the bodhisattva as the
central personage. The bodhisattva works for the salvation of
mankind as a whole rather than for his "own" salvation. His is
a life of sacrifice. The bodhisattva dramatizes the contrast we
have been discussing between professional and lay Buddhism,
and is a means of overcoming it. Mahayana, like Christianity,
acknowledges human weakness. One cannot expect much of
men, even when the stakes are eternal bliss. In both cases an
intercessor and a savior are needed, someone who will do for
man what man is too debased to do for himself. Now, in a
way, the two sides of Buddhism are reconciled.

The general conception of the bodhisattva is that of one
who has attained enlightenment and can pass over into Nirvana, but who postpones his own bliss until all mankind has
reached the same point as he—and then all will pass over together. In fact, this description is somewhat vulgar. For by the
same logic that negates the *arhat*, the position of the bodhisattva just described is also impossible. There is an interesting
moral paradox. The bodhisattva cannot pass over into Nirvana.
He cannot because, were he to do so he would exhibit a selfishness that a bodhisattva cannot have. If he has the selfishness,
he is not a bodhisattva, and so cannot enter Nirvana. If he
lacks the selfishness, again, he cannot enter Nirvana, for that
would be a selfish act. So either way, the bodhisattva is impotent to enter Nirvana. Like God who, in the Christian teaching, cannot do evil because it is inconsistent with his nature,
the bodhisattva cannot perform the ultimately selfish act. So
no one can reach Nirvana: *we* cannot because we are not bodhisattvas, and the bodhisattva cannot because he is a bodhisattva. But in fact, so long as we acknowledge a difference
amongst ourselves, we are implicitly acknowledging the existence of selves, and so craving, and so are held to life. Only
when there are no distinctions between selves will craving

cease: and with the cessation of craving comes Nirvana. Light exists only when there is dark. When all the dark goes, all the light goes as well. This is the sense of Nirvana in the Mahayana system.

The bodhisattva is not required to perform acts of goodwill. Certain bodhisattvas, of course, play this sort of role in popular mythology. The delightful Kuan Yin is Heeder of the Cries of the World. Mortals call upon her at times of desperation. She (or he—Kuan Yin is sexually ambiguous) is like the Virgin Mary, the soft-heart and ready sympathizer, and able to work miracles. There is a whole genre of Buddhist art in which Kuan Yin is there to rescue the drowning, heal the sick, and break the executioner's sword before it severs the victim's head. Typically, however, the bodhisattva is an exemplar to the world rather than a ministering merciful angel. He provides a certain still moral center, and serves as a paradigm and an anchor. He need but follow the Eightfold Path, in which the strand of right contemplation, characteristic of India, is the chief one.

The statues of Buddha and of the bodhisattvas show deeply peaceful personages, turned inward upon themselves, fixed centers of unshakable beatitude. They are like rocks in the swirling world. The opposition between their imperturbability and our own frantic lives is shattering. It is hard to endure that much peace. One thinks of Rainer Maria Rilke's response to the torso of an antique apollo: *"Du muss dein Leben ändern."* It is through just being himself that the bodhisattva does what is required and as much, perhaps, as is possible. For only when we see ourselves in the contrast he thrusts upon us, in our weakness and hopelessness, will we perhaps begin to break the ties that hold us to the mad world. And to find not the peace we thirst for but the peace from thirst (which is synonymous with 'craving' in the Buddhist lexicon) itself. The bodhisattva produces peace through peace. The appeal, at times, is overwhelming. But it usually does not last. The world reasserts itself and our resolutions dissolve. We sink again into the red dust. So the Mahayana ideal comes to seem all the more hopeless, edifying and universal as it is. Nirvana is hopelessly remote. If a man who is a bodhisattva, or appears to be one, should emerge in one of our communities—and there are, after all, men of genuine religious talent—we would recognize him, no doubt, and at the same time recognize the immense distance between him and us. We no more could be like him through practice than we could be like the piano virtuoso through dint of hard work. If we are Orientals, we will explain his facility in terms of his accumulated propitious karma, and our incapacities in the same way. We are separated from the bodhisattva by a moral space so immense that it would require uncountably many karmic appearances to close it. So the mitigating dynamisms of Mahayana leave just the same cleavage between the expert and the layman as before. The promised peace is as far away as ever. And the human weakness that Mahayana was to help man overcome asserts itself again.

This disproportion between expert and layman was exploited as a dynamic in Buddhism's transformation from a therapy to a religion, which is in large measure what Mahayana is. To begin with, Buddha himself increasingly came to be seen not as just another man, but as a being with singular prerogatives. To begin with, he did not hesitate to enter Nirvana. The great perhaps are always exempt from rules that are binding upon everyone else: the breaking of the rules that mark the common practitioner as a bungler serves to emphasize the genius of the great. Here, again, we find an evidence of the antinomianism of the religious hero, who does not himself follow the path he shows. In time the Buddha is promoted to the status of a god. And it is at that point that human weakness, on the one side, coupled with the divinity of the Buddha figure, on the other, transforms the teaching into a salvational faith.

The *Lotus Sutra* impresses one by the use it makes of immensities. It refers to unimaginably large periods of time and expanses of space; it refers to worlds beyond worlds, and ages behind ages. There are visions of the Buddha's avatars in staggeringly remote Buddha-worlds and Buddha-ages. Our span is puny. Our power dwindles to impotency in the face of this awesome vastness. The *Lotus Sutra* is a reducing mechanism: it forces one to see oneself as laughably minute and irrelevant. It is a prodigious literary technique, and it would be a demoralizing one as well, were it not for the hopes it offers. These hopes become increasingly attainable as our own power for attaining them decreases. Salvation becomes easy. We need but read the *Lotus*. Or not even that. We need only call upon the Buddha, and we are saved. Nothing less powerful than this multidimensional, unimaginably vast being, whom the Buddha has become in proportion to the minuscule being that is man, could counteract the factors that make for hopelessness in the world and by simple means redeem us. But in all of this the Eightfold Path has faded. The discipline of the monk is not needed. The renunciatory effort need no longer be made. Merely call upon the Buddha-God: and that is enough. Buddha will save.

Of course, the *Nembutsu*—the call to Buddha—does not guarantee nirvanic salvation. Sometimes only an intermediate salvation is promised, say rebirth in a Pure Land, the land of Amidha Buddha. This has great appeal, quite naturally. In Japan it became a dominating faith. Lovers, who have found the world inhospitable to their passion, have performed aesthetic love-suicides; at the final moment as they called upon Buddha, they were certain in their hearts that instantly they would be reborn together on a lotus leaf in the Pure Land. The Pure Land is only a way station to the higher, nirvanic bliss. It is assumed that later, one will try for something higher. But it satisfies the concrete mentality of the normally weak, as it would yours and mine. Most of us would prefer a paradise we can imagine to the thin bliss of vacuity. Vacuity is what most of us fear.

Buddhism polarizes into a popular religion with easily attainable and extraordinary goals, on the one hand, and into a difficult intellectual and mystical theology, on the other. All the great religions are hospitable to these extremes. Christianity has room for Saint Thomas and for Santa Claus; Islam houses Averroes and those who believe in a heaven of gazelle-eyed houris in whose laps the devout will know a sexual bliss that even the best in this world could only palely foreshadow. Nevertheless, there is in Buddhism an attempt to synthesize these extremes, and in a way that clearly shows its Indian pedigree. It is the high Vedantic teaching that the world is *Brahma* so that one's flight from the world to *Brahma* is in the end a flight to the world, but to the world seen in a different light and under a different perspective. In this perspective, one at the same time lives in the world and does not. Buddhism, too, comes to teach that the *Samsara* world, thought to be distinct from Nirvana, is really Nirvana. Nirvana is here. It is in this spirit that a Zen monk, reprimanded for spitting upon a statue of the Buddha, replied that since Buddha was everywhere, it is impossible to spit and not spit on Buddha. When the *Samsara* world is made Nirvana, it is equally impossible not to be saved whatever one does: even if one just eats and sleeps. This teaching I should like to discuss, for it brings us to an aspect of Oriental thought that is distinctive and important to our purpose.

When the distinction between the *samsara* world, the perpetual cycle of rebirth, and Nirvana is collapsed, our daily life is stained with religious significance. The entirety of life is religious, rather than a restricted portion of it reserved for ritual and specific observances marked out as "religious." Everything we do becomes a religious act, even, to use the example cited a moment ago, eating and sleeping. Can religion be that simple? In one sense, yes; in another, no. For most of us do not eat and sleep in the consciousness of them as religious acts. A religious act is not one of a special class of acts, but an act performed with a certain attitude and through a certain perspective. So we need not change our practices in any way, only the spirit in which we pursue them. It is instructive to think in this connection of a distinction that has very recently been blurred, the distinction between art works and ordinary objects: it has been found that ordinary objects can be art works without undergoing any internal modification—that art works and ordinary objects are the same things, though grouped in different ways and appreciated in a different spirit. The whole world can become aestheticized without there being any change in the world at all.

In a way, one can think of Nietzsche's *amor fati* ("love of fate") doctrine in this connection. *Amor fati* is the key to a release from the bondage of one's destiny, for by affirming what one does, by endorsing it, one makes it one's own. The content of our actions has not changed. Only the light in which we perform acts has altered making the difference between freedom and bondage. In one way, nothing is changed. But in another way, everything is changed. It is in this way that the *samsara* world become the nirvana world without any alteration. To do what we always do in this way is at once to be within the world and without the world: to be in and beyond the world at once.

Whether or not this is a formula for salvation, it is not bad as a formula for attaining happiness. According to it, this world is the only world, salvation not consisting in the transcendence of this world into a world beyond, but in accepting this world as sanctified. What is called for, is not a transformation of the world, but a transformation of the vision of ourselves and our relation to the world. So in doing our "thing," as it has become fashionable to say, we each attain the salvation we seek.

This is a teaching it is difficult not to respect. But I do not believe it will do as a moral philosophy. Since it permits the ritualization of everything, every act can be interpreted as a religious discipline, such as the manufacture of instruments of torture, the skills involved in bringing the maximum of exquisite agony to one's victim. One of the great logical insights of Socrates was that every skill, every "thing" can be used or abused, the same skills that enable one to win a race enable one, as a positive achievement, to lose a race as well. It was this insight that led him to seek a moral knowledge that could not be reduced to the various sorts of knowledge in which the possession of skills consists. Nor will the doing of one's "thing" selflessly and impersonally make an act "good": for it was the boast of such figures as Adolf Eichmann, for example, that he was only doing his thing. Finally, if the *samsara* world is the Nirvana world, whatever exists in one exists in the other, and the conditions that occasioned us to relinquish desire and repress craving in order to surmount suffering could only assert themselves in the same way as before. And some way has to be found for rationalizing evil.

Ethics has to do with how we should treat one another, not merely with how we are to treat ourselves alone. Devotion to our *dharma*, appropriate and selfless execution of our tasks, while it may promote or even constitute salvation, is neither sufficient nor even necessary as a minimal ethical requirement. To be sure, Buddhism as a religion is concerned with salvation. But we can see that the demands of salvation and the demands of morality are not automatically and simultaneously fulfilled, and they may even be antithetical. Morality cannot be a technique of salvation, even if the same acts that are moral are the same ones that entail salvation. The fact that they lead to salvation cannot constitute a moral justification.

This is not to say that Buddhism is lacking in moral rules. It is only that they are not internal to the theory of Buddhism. The monk is subject to a number of prohibitions, such as being forbidden to murder or to be involved in murder in any way. It is characteristic of Buddhism's charm that one of its cardinal sins is to claim supernormal powers. The humanity of the Buddha shines through the features of the institutions he generated, even if his thought was to degenerate into a religion like the rest.

THE DISCIPLINE OF ACTION
IN THE *Bhagavad Gita*

The taste for immensities, to which I alluded in my remarks on the *Lotus Sutra,* and which, I believe, is representative of the Indian sensibility, is hardly more conspicuously exhibited than in the great Indian epics, and especially in the *Mahabarata.* This work which is often advertised as eight times the length of the *Iliad* and *Odyssey* combined—"It is," Professor K. Irani once said, "an experience merely to see it on the book shelf."—has a unifying narrative thread which holds together an otherwise heterogeneous mass of legends and poems. Many of the pieces included seemed to have somehow gotten lodged in the epic and remained. The narrative concerns the adventures of five brothers—one might almost say that it has a pentadic hero—all of whom are consistently married to the same woman, Draupadi. The focus of the story concerns their right to a kingdom, which is contested by the jealous and, on the whole, inferior Kaurava cousins. The five Pandava brothers are required, in standard epic format, to undergo a series of trials and ultimately a series of crushingly savage battles—in effect, a civil war—before they attain their patrimony. What makes the epic characteristically Indian is that the heroes at last weary of life and seek salvation. After another series of trials, they, along with their wife and the eldest brother's dog, attain it.

The *Mahabarata* is a repository of moral instruction and a chivalric code. It furnishes paradigms for moral guidance, much as the Greek epics did, and played a corresponding role in moral education. Our concern, however, is with the great *Bhagavad Gita* (the *Song of the Lord*) which is inserted into the epic at the point where the major deciding battles are to be fought. The two sides are drawn up in opposition, awaiting the commencement of combat. One of the Pandava brothers, Arjuna, the bowman, instructs his charioteer to drive up and down the neutral strip between the two armies. The driver is a friendly prince, Krishna, who reveals himself in the course of this reconnoiter, which is more moral than military, as the Lord Vishnu. Before the expedition is done Arjuna knows the meaning of life and the nature of god. Hence the title of the work. The symbolism of the lord-chariot driver is striking and profound, and the poetic body of the *Gita* does not fall beneath the level of imagination the symbolism establishes. It is a literary and philosophical masterpiece, a permanently self-renewing work of the highest order, and a contribution to the spiritual consciousness of mankind.

The war about to be fought will not be between anonymous enemies. Lined up against Arjuna's people are cousins and uncles, teachers and childhood friends. "How, having slain our kinsfold/Could we be happy?" Arjuna asks (1:39). "Even if *they* do not see/Because their intelligence is destroyed by greed,/The sin caused by destruction of the family/And the crime involved in injury to a friend/How should *we* not know enough/To turn back from this wickedness . . . ?" Arjuna is not merely distressed by the infraction of a code of conduct, as a knight might be. Rather, he sees a chain of consequences leading to moral disaster. If the "immemorially holy laws of family" are violated, what laws will be respected? His argument here is that if a man would not hesitate to break these laws, he will not hesitate to break any. This is not, as we shall see, merely a fear that a kind of dam will be broken and that lawlessness will flood the land. Arjuna, and the Indians generally, did not attach conservative priority to the preservation of law as law. In the *Ramayana* (*Life of Rama*), the companion epic, the hero and heroine are so morally upright as to verge upon vapidness, and their trials are consequences of their scorn of expediencies. To be sure, they are moral paradigms, and the logic of paradigms is such that they who violate the law lose their status as paradigms and the law in question goes empty. A special code of rectitude devolves, after all, upon moral teachers and exemplars, and children are absolutely right in regarding their parent's hypocrisy in moral matters as a serious dereliction, considerably graver than the particular deviation involved—say, dishonesty or adultery—for these, while deplorable enough, are moral departures that at least leave the structure of morality intact. But when teachers, as authorities on moral matters, engage in the practices they officially condemn, the sources of morality are made inconsistent and the system of morality becomes incoherent. We have a special obligation to morality as such, which differs in logical kind from any specific moral obligations: and in the case of teachers and parents, or rulers such as Rama and Sita, a moral lapse is a lapse of morality.

For Arjuna, however, it is not the collapse of morality that is fazing. For morality, in his implicit view, is woven with the fabric of the world, and his reasoning is the following. If lawlessness reigns, the women of the family will be corrupted, and will sleep with whom they will. There will then be mixtures of caste. When castes are corrupted, the rituals are not kept as they should be. Rituals performed by those not qualified, viz; other than *Brahmans*, are invalid or worse. Given the potencies attributed to correctly performed rituals in keeping the forces of nature in harmony, one can see that the chaos envisaged by Arjuna transcends moral anarchy. So he decides he will not fight. He would rather perish than contribute to the degeneration of the universe.

Arjuna is caught in a moral conflict: a collision of two codes. If he fights in this war, he breaks the code of the family, with the consequences sketched: consequences he cannot seriously doubt without more or less doubting everything, since all his beliefs are based on revelation. If, however, he does not fight, he violates another code, that of the *Kshatriya*, and he will be a bad knight. Either way, and the option is a forced one, he is in moral discredit. Still, he argues, the responsibilities of fratricide would be so onerous as to be insupportable, even though he should personally profit and reign over gods and men. Krishna, "with the semblance of a smile," then sets out a series of arguments designed to dissolve the dilemma. And in the course of this discourse, he reveals his divinity, announces the incorruptibility of the soul, and finally lays down a series of directives for the attainment of salvation. Thus, it was inevitable that the *Gita* acquire the status of a scripture and, as such, play a huge structuring role in the evolution of Indian society.

Krishna utters these celebrated words: "Thou hast mourned those who should not be mourned" (II:ii). The wise do not mourn men, for men do not die: they but interchange one life for another. "Not at any moment was I (ever) not,/Nor thou, nor these kings. / And not at all shall we ever come not to be. / . . . The embodied soul is eternally unslayable / In the body of every one . . ." (II: 12, 30). This is a radical teaching. It means, in effect, that if Arjuna wished to kill anyone he could not (really) succeed. This, of course, detaches one's homicidal acts from a certain chain of consequences. It could be argued that the point is irrelevant, since it is not in terms of such considerations that we think of murder to begin with: but if we had the assurance that upon being killed, a man would instantly attain a state of beatitude, we no doubt would have to change our own views on killing. It might, for example, be a form of capital punishment to keep a person alive. It is only because we believe otherwise that we hold to the set of moral beliefs that certainly would lose application were our factual beliefs concerning death different. There is another point implicit in

Krishna's revelation: it is that they, being lodged in the bodies they occupy, are no more really members of a family that their bodies bore them into than they really are the bodies themselves. So you would not be killing anyone who is really a member of your family. At any rate, the point is general: there is no final death, and hence no death: "Therefore, all beings thou shouldst not mourn" (II: 30).

On the other hand, it is the specific duty of the warrior to fight. Only by fighting, Arjuna is assured, do warriors attain salvation. If Arjuna does not fight, therefore, he will be disgraced amongst men and penalized in the karmic order. If he fights, "Either slain, thou shalt gain heaven / Or conquering, thou shalt enjoy the earth" (II: 36). So sophistical an argument is perhaps unbecoming to a god (although Krishna has not yet disclosed his divine identity), and it is inconsistent with, or at least must be revised in the light of, the theses he advances a moment later. These will prove to be the central teaching of the *Gita:* "On action alone be thy interest, / Never on its fruits" (II: 47). Surely in some sense it is in terms of advantageous consequences that Krishna's first argument is expressed, but the injunction to focus all one's concern upon the act remains the distinctive doctrine of the *Gita*. For as it transpires, it is precisely through accepting it that one will "get rid of the bondage of action" (II:39), which is to say *karma*.

Let me interpret this thought against the background of Indian beliefs. Recall that, in theory, our *karma* is determined by our actions, and, hence, what we are and what we will be must be understood as the consequence of what we have done and what we do. It follows from this that if we could act inconsequentially, there would be no *karma* whatever. So, by actionlessness we could escape the wheel of life and death and life and death. Something like this is often implicit in the quietistic techniques of Indian asceticism. The Jain recommend death through starvation as a way out of *karma*. The yoga go into increasingly protracted periods of inanition. And there is

a general and almost overwhelming propensity, as the underside of Indian practice, to attain a state of apathy, or actionlessness, in such a way that one passes a lifetime without doing
anything. One lives off of stored *karma*, so to speak, without
acquiring any *karma* further. One task of the *Gita* appears to
have been to combat this tendency. "A body bearing soul," it
says, "cannot abandon actions without remainder" (XVIII: 11).
We are through our nature under a necessity always to be acting, roughly in the way in which, according to Descartes, we
are, through our essence as *res cogitans*, under a necessity always to be thinking: *"l'âme pense toujours."* Just as it is impossible to stop thinking—one can only have different
thoughts—so it is impossible to stop acting—one can only
act in a different way. There is, after all, a profound difference
between not doing *a* and doing *not-a;* and to believe that
doing *not-a* is not doing anything, is as fallacious as the inference that if one knows that it is not raining, one has no knowledge. In Cartesian terms, thinking about nothing is still thinking. "Not by not starting actions/ Does a man attain/
actionlessness/And not by renunciation alone/Does he go to
perfection. For no one even for a moment/Remains at all
without performing actions . . ." (II: 4–5). In other words,
desisting from action, or forbearance, is itself an action, for
only agents may forbear, and forbearance is one form of
agency. Forbearance, then, is no less an action for being negative, and it is not obviously a *karma*-aborting action. Since we
must act, escape from *karma*, if possible, must lie in other
directions. It is against this background that one must appreciate Krishna's first responses to Arjuna. Just as it is our nature
to act, so that we cannot consistently with our nature not act;
so—though in a weaker sense—it is deeply unnatural for a
warrior, who is born a warrior, not to fight when the opportunity arises. It would be contrary to his nature and karmically
damning for Arjuna not to fight. Since he must do something,
the thing to do is what he is suited to do. It is not fighting but

the attitude towards fighting that is the important thing, and once that is made clear, Arjuna, or anyone, will be able to act in such a way as to avoid *karma* completely. This is obviously an important revelation, given the preoccupations of Hinduism, for it suggests a way of reaching salvation through action.

The *Gita* lays out three distinct paths to salvation. One of these is the path, or discipline, of action: the so-called karma-yoga. There is also the path of devotion (*bhakti*) and the path of knowledge. The path of knowledge, we are already familiar with: knowledge has traditionally been *the* path to salvation in India. Not unnaturally, it is given a certain priority in the *Gita*, but the crucial consideration is that the *Gita* opens and acknowledges other paths. This is very important socially. It marks an opening downward in the caste-scale, enabling members of the *Kshatriya* caste to attain salvation directly and by means appropriate to them, rather than have to await rebirth as a *Brahman*. Meanwhile, it keeps the prerogatives and privileges of brahmahood supreme. But none of this is internally represented in the concept of redemption through action, so let us return to that.

One cannot forbear from acting, though one can forbear from a given action. Total inactivity is not something that we can achieve so long as we are as we are—"body-bearing souls." But what we can do, according to the *Gita*, is to detach ourselves from our acts: as the commentators say, it is not *naiskarmya* (negation of action), but *niskama karma* (detached action) that the *Gita* enjoins. "The abandonment of all action-fruits / The wise call abandonment," it says; and again "But he who abandons the fruit of action / is called the man of [true] abandonment," and finally "On action alone by thy interest / Never on its fruits; / Let not the fruits of action be thy motive, / Nor be thy attachment to inaction." Krishna says: "Discipline is defined as indifference."

Now though a difficult teaching to follow, this is not hard to understand. Essentially, a man who follows the discipline

puts himself outside the scope of the standard question we almost always feel justified in asking of one who performs an action, namely, why is he doing it? This "why" is by no means
simple to analyze, as readers of G. E. M. Anscombe's book *Intention* will recognize. Chiefly, however, answers that have the
form "in order to" or "in order that" are responses to "why,"
and what the *Gita* wants to rule out is a special subclass of
such answers. It would allow, for example, a baker answer-
ing "Why are you putting that yeast in with the flour?" with
"In order that the dough will rise," but not "Why are you
baking that cake?" with "In order to win the blue ribbon."
What the *Gita* wants is that the baker should bake cakes
without caring whether or not they win blue ribbons, but one
could not bake cakes not caring whether they rise or not. In
the latter case, he does not care whether or not he is a
cook, which is not what the *Gita* wants. In the first case he
does not care whether he is recognized or rewarded for his
culinary art, and it is this attitude particularly that the *Gita*
charges us to acquire. If one is a cook—or a warrior like Arjuna, or whatever—one has a primary obligation to perform
those actions commensurate to one's calling, but winning blue
ribbons is not part of baking successfully, any more than winning kingdoms is part of fighting effectively, or gaining Nobel
prizes is part of scientific work. What this means, basically, is
that the *Gita* wants us to behave unmotivatedly, not to have
motives for what one does, but only to do what one does because that is the way to do what it is one's nature to do. The
correct or acceptable answer to "Why are you doing that?" if
what one is seeking is not instruction in how things are done,
is more or less this: "I am a *C* and this is what *C*'s do." If I am
a *C*, my obligation is to fulfill *C*-hood, but *I* have no motives
over and above this for doing what I do. Indian thought makes
a good deal of this, and ascribes an immense power to persons
who become one with their calling: a standard moral heroine,
for example, is the disinterested prostitute, who exercises her

calling in so disinterested a manner that she acquires a personal force vast enough to cause the Ganges river to flow backwards. "Free alike from fawning and from dislike do I do service to him who has bought me," says a remarkable whore in the *Milinda Panya* (*Questions of King Menander*). "This . . . is the basis of the Act of Truth by the force of which I turned the Ganges back."

Up to a point, I think, we can all appreciate this notion of disinterested action. For example, it would be considered morally blameworthy to have motives for certain of the actions we perform. An innocuous enough example of this is being polite. If a man acknowledges the question "Why are you being polite?" as appropriate, he automatically places himself in a dubious moral light: having a motive is wrong, independent of what the motive might be if one had one. Here the correct answer might be "I am a civilized person, and civilized persons are polite"—rather than, for example, "For no reason at all." For the latter implies the legitimacy of "For *this* reason." This does not mean that a sociological explanation of politeness would be ruled out as a reason why *one* is polite. But I think that what we have in mind in discrediting motives in connection with politeness is more or less our view that reference to motives for behavior is actually reference to a necessary condition, and the implication is that had the person not had a motive for being polite, he would not have been polite; and, therefore, would not meet the standard of behavior we universally demand of "civilized" persons. There are other examples. We in some measure disrespect artists who paint pictures merely for money or who paint, or writers write, for any reason other than producing works of art. We expect, or our myths lead to expect, a certain purity of soul: we feel there is something utterly appropriate in Paul Cezanne wandering off, leaving his paintings abandoned in the land around Aix, not at all caring whether or not they were shown or whether he was rewarded or not. By contrast, think of Nietzsche's disillusionment with Richard Wagner ("human, all-too-human"), or our own suspicions about professionalism in sports: people should climb mountains because they are mountain climbers, for the sake of the thing itself and nothing ulterior. Insofar as we think in this manner, we are thinking in harmony with the *Gita*.

It is, of course, exceedingly difficult to think of behaving in this impersonal way all of the time, becoming coincident, as I have put it, with one's role. And, to show the other side of the coin, we hold it against people who *are* utterly impersonal in their dealings, who identify with their offices: we say they are not human, are mere machines, or have no heart. One sees this type of person over and over again in the Indian stories: heroes and heroines in the great epics, for example, seem to have no inside, are completely on the surface, like a moral möbius strip: Rama is purely and wholly a king, Sita purely and wholly a wife. One finds none of the complexity of motive and feeling for interiority with which we are so much concerned in our own literature, and which even our epic heroes, like Achilles and Ulysses, exhibit to a singular degree. Western heroes have "personalities," which the Indian ones lack. But we must not forget that it is the loss of individuality that constitutes salvation in the Indian schema, and the karma-yoga is a way of living as though one were disconnected, given that one must always be acting.

It is not easy to say why the karma-yoga should serve to neutralize *karma*, but perhaps the thesis is the following. If I detach myself from the consequences of an action through withdrawal of care or concern, then the consequences somehow are not mine. They are caused by what I do, but I do not do what I do in order that they should happen. Since they are not mine, I am not affected by them. The metaphysical picture that goes with this is more or less as follows. I am an indestructible self. I am lodged in a body, which is just the body I deserve to be lodged in in virtue of the way I have behaved in the past bodies assigned to me. This will go on until I recognize the fundamental distinction between myself and my body. What concern is it to me what happens to, or because of, my body? The body is in a causal order, and all manner of consequences flow forth from its behavior in that order. These consequences would be mine if I were closely identified with my body. But I am not. By distinguishing between self and body, Krishna makes it possible to detach oneself intellectually, and ultimately existentially, from the body's consequences, all the while acting in conformity with the nature of the body one is in.

One's body is always an anomaly in Eastern thinking. One is stuck with the body, or with a body, and has to act with it, even if it does not belong essentially to one's self. And the problem of finding the right attitude towards this alien crass object always arises. Obviously, one has a most intimate connection with it, however embarrassing this may be. Part of the healthiness of the *Gita* is that it suggests that since we have a body, we had better act in a way that acknowledges its nature. In the *Milinda Panya*, the sage Nagasena is asked by the King whether he loves his body, which Nagasena denies. In that case, why treat it so well: why feed and cosset it? Is this not inconsistent, is not the whole parade of other-worldly sentiment hypocritical? Ought not one do the brutal but obvious thing? Nagasena has a cagey answer. The King surely has suffered a wound? And has bandaged the wound, and treated it with unguents? Is this because the King loved his wound? No. One does not love the body. But one can be detached from it. The alternatives are not self-brutalization or self-indulgence. The *Gita*, too, provides a middle way.

Not to care, I think, and this is a problem with the *Gita* as a moral tract, verges on not being quite human. There is something chilling in the image that the *Gita* creates as we approach the end: Krishna, "The Lord of Discipline," and Arjuna the Bowman cease their colloquy and revert to their momentary essences. Now they move through the battle with that half smile of the inturned face of Indian art as they slay their way dispassionately across the field of conflict, as though they were cutting their way with scythes through a field of wheat. It is not a pretty picture. It is a picture, however, of a self that has located itself beyond good and evil. That is a dangerous space. It has been occupied by Nietzsche's Superman and by those who thought of themselves as Supermen. It is not a moral stand, but a stand outside morality, and while salvation may indeed lie in that direction, this only would underscore what we must regard as a conflict between religion and morality. But perhaps this dramatizes the respect in which the concept of morality rests on factual premises radically at odds with the premises of the *Gita*.

The *Gita* contains a great deal of practical moral advice, including, paradoxically, an injunction against violence. But actions performed in accordance with the Discipline of Action are, by the criterion of the *Gita* itself, beyond good and evil and, so, beyond moral appraisal, which is concerned with whether an act may be said to be good or evil. When I say that acts are beyond good and evil, I do not mean that the very same acts, from an external point of view, might not be good or evil: the goodness or badness of an action by the *Gita*'s criterion is very much a matter of the context in which the act is embedded, rather than a matter of anything intrinsic to the act as such.

For one thing, the Discipline of Action removes an action from one context we ordinarily use to appraise an action: the context of its consequences. Here the teaching of the *Gita* connects with a superficially similar and central teaching of Kant. Kant argued that however disastrous or beneficent the consequences of an action may be, they should not be considered in the moral appraisals of the action itself. Kant has been widely and famously disputed on this point, and although

there are important schools of moral philosophy that are defined specifically through the fact that the moral value of an
action is determined by its consequences, I, nevertheless, feel
that Kant reflects our common practice in these matters. This
has to be of some weight in assessing the viability of a moral
philosophy, for after all, it is we who make moral judgments.
By our common practice here, I mean: of an action that has
unpleasant or untoward consequences, we may say that it was
a bad thing that it happened; and of an action with pleasant or
felicitous consequences, we may say it was a good thing that it
happened. Still, though the action may be a good or bad event,
in these terms, it is so only in the way that rainfall would be a
good or bad event—relative to our needs and wants. Yet, it
by no means follows that it is good or bad in the morally relevant senses of "good" and "bad." It is good or bad in a nonmoral sense of these terms. To be sure, it might be argued, few
could deny that if we did only those things that conduced to
the general welfare and avoided those things that were antithetical to it, other criteria for evaluating human actions would
become decreasingly relevant. But even so, the fact is that we
do distinguish a moral sense of "good," which Utilitarianism
has not so much given an analysis of, but rather, by the
argument just sketched, has hoped to substitute with its own
commendable usage. My inclination is to believe that Utilitarianism hoped that the moral sense of "good" would come to
apply only to those actions that are "good" in the specifically
nonmoral sense: but it would be sheer good luck if it worked
out that way, and an analysis of "goods" moral sense would still
be needed. Kant held that the criteria for the moral sense of the
term were such that consequences were irrelevant to its application. And in some sense, surely, he is right: an act of murder
is not bad because of its consequences, but, one feels, for some
more absolute reason.

To begin with, there cannot be a moral use of terms unless
there are some systems of rules. Consider, for a moment, steal-

ing. Nobody can both understand the word "stealing" and, at the same time, believe that stealing is morally all right. To steal, for example, is to take something to which one has no right, knowing that one has no right to it. I may take something to which I have no right but not know that I have no right to it, in which case it would not be stealing. So knowing that it is stealing is part of the action of stealing. But further, I cannot know this unless there are rules that define the notion of right of ownership. It was Hobbes' great insight that theft is not a "natural" event, though the physical pre-emption of a hide or of a woman is natural enough. In a state of nature, to use his famous expression, there is no property: one can only steal where there is property, and there is property only where there is a system of rules, and there is a system of rules only in a state. In the state of nature, everyone has a right to everything, which, in effect, is to say that there are no property rights at all. Now a man may say that property itself ought not to exist, that "property is theft," to use Proudhon's slogan, an incoherent one, since if there is no property, there logically could be no theft. But my point is that you cannot know what stealing means and say that "stealing" is morally all right. There is always the question of whether a man has taken or stolen something, the difference lying not in the event itself, but in the man who performed the action. It is not just a question of whether he intended the action, for there remains a difference between intending to take and intending to steal. I may take something I have no right to, thinking I do have a right to it or thinking it a different object than it is. In that case, I did not steal: I only took it illegally: I *took* intentionally, but did not *steal* intentionally, and so did not steal at all. But from this line of analysis it follows that there is no such thing as stealing unintentionally, and what makes the difference between taking and stealing is the agent's intention. This comes close to Kant's theory that it is the will with which an action is done that determines the moral quality of the act. But of course this is only a necessary condition, there being, as I have suggested, more to the matter than this.

Now, I think one reason that we make this reference to intention—one reason that we cannot judge the moral quality of an action until we can describe the action in relation to the agent's knowledge and intention—is that our main interest lies not so much in the action as in the agent, who is its originator, and our concern is basically to determine whether the action is *his* according to the description we just gave. The act is his under the description "taking x" but perhaps not his under the description "stealing x" even though, outwardly, there is nothing to distinguish the two cases. Our aim in moral judgment is to connect in some deep internal way the agent with his actions. One way, certainly, to escape moral censure is to be able to show that the action in question is not yours, at least under a description that carries blameworthiness. Of course, if no action is yours in this sense, you never do anything to which any moral value is attached. You behave in a morally neutral way. Someone who has not learned that there is a difference between right and wrong would always be morally neutral in this way, or amoral, and would effectively live in Hobbes' state of nature. And the bearing of all of this on the *Gita* lies in this: the directives of the *Gita* towards the karma-yoga serve to neutralize the moral qualities of one's actions by making the actions *not yours*. For the entire burden of the Discipline of Action is to achieve detachment from one's actions. Arjuna's actions are, in the morally relevant sense, not his. And they not being his, *he*, of course, is exempted from any moral penalties in the karmic order. In what sense, then, is it true that *we* are always acting?

There is a sense in which we may think of this. Those events in our history are not ours, in the morally relevant sense, which follow from our nature when our nature is understood in rather a special way. For this sense, one may turn to Nietzsche. Nietzsche believed that we make a fundamental error in believing implicitly that there is a subject distinct from actions that performs the actions. When we think in these terms, it seems logical that the subject can either perform them or not, the doing or not doing being somehow up to him. But lightning, Nietzsche argues, is not something distinct from the flashing, which has the option to flash or not. Lightning *is* the flashing. And Nietzsche believed that the fact that we have a subject-predicate grammar has misled us into believing that we live in a subject-predicate world. I shall not comment on this, except to suggest that it is in just this sense that Krishna apparently meant his statement that it is the nature, or the essence, of a *Kshatriya* to fight. He must fight because it is his nature. It would require a complex analysis to sort out what manner of confusion Arjuna, according to this theory, has been in. He has supposed he was identical with the bowman, and had the option of fighting or not. But in fact he is detached, as a self, from the bowman which is only his momentary abode. The bowman he is attached to has no choice, it being its nature to fight, as it is the nature of lightning to flash. In other words, Arjuna is at once within and without the karmic world. Because he is without it, what happens in it issuing from his body is not his. And because what is in it has a certain nature, and so must do certain things, then what happens in consequence of this nature is not his either. So nothing he does is really his, providing only he realizes this. Then, it is ignorance of his relation to his body, and of his body's relation to its acts, that makes these actions seem to be his, and so keeps him chained to the karmic order. Characteristically, ignorance is what keeps us chained to the world, and release is through knowledge, in this case knowledge of my self and of the nature of my body (in the broad sense that "body" includes its caste qualifications). Through ignorance, Arjuna thinks he is his body and has the option of doing with his body what he wishes, viz, fighting or not. And so he acts in an unnatural way and is, therefore, damned to repeat and repeat his acts until he realizes the metaphysical truth. And then he is free.

There is much to criticize in this, but I am less interested now in the philosophical difficulties of the account—and let us remember that the *Gita* is a song and not a treatise—than I am in the Oriental notion of man's *nature*, which we are given and with which we ought not to interfere. Salvation lies in attaining congruity with our nature in the sense of not obscuring or obstructing it. This suggests that something unnatural can happen, and so this theory is different, after all, from Nietzsche's thesis, according to which lightning cannot at once be lightning and not flash. Arjuna can "not-fight," but it is contrary to his nature. At this point it occurs to one that *karma* accrues primarily through acting unnaturally, or contrary to nature, since what happens naturally is something that follows from our nature and is not ours. It is a striking thought that we are responsible only for our counter-natural behavior. It is interfering with nature that causes trouble, and with this I wish to turn to ancient China, where we find a theory that helps illuminate karma-yoga, almost as though the one were a resonance of the other.

CONFORMING TO THE WAY

The great philosophical poem, *Tao Te Ching*, which according to legend was authored by Lao Tzu, "The Old Man," and which is the canonical document of Taoism as a religion, begins with this verse: "The way that can be told of is not the real way." One senses immediately that the Taoists had a certain distrust of verbalization and, in a way, a general mistrust of the intellect—or what we might term the discursive intellect, since it is this intellect that is concerned with representing in words or their counterparts the way the world is. Often, when Westerners turn to the Orient for spiritual guidance or refreshment, it is just this mistrust that attracts them, even though the idea that language is a distorting lens, and that reality, in relationship to it, is ineffable is a concept that is also known in the West. However reality is to be grasped, words will not serve. Such was Bergson's view, and such has been the view of mystics and hippies, ancient and contemporary. It merits a comment, I believe, before we address the *Tao*, or the Way.

It is a striking fact that philosophers have often acted as though, in order for the world to be put into language and described, the structure of the world must be antecedently linguistic. The most recent exemplar of this view, Ludwig Wittgenstein, advanced in his *Tractatus* the theory that propositions and facts must share a certain "logical form," if the former are to describe the latter. To be sure Wittgenstein believed that in an ideal sense a proposition is a picture of a fact. Since resemblance at some level is criterial for pictures, and since, again, nothing could superficially less resemble a dog scratching than the proposition that the dog is scratching, the demand for resemblance that the pictorial relation imposed required some sort of parity, which Wittgenstein identified as "logical form." It is not as though every metaphysician who has construed reality as shaped by logical form—as having a linguistic structure at its heart—has explicitly endorsed the pictorial theory of description. But claims regarding the ineffability of reality often enough have been based on the denial that reality has the form of language, a reasonable enough denial except that to ground ineffability upon it is to commit the same fallacy, namely, to hold that reality is linguistically graspable only if it *is* costructural with its descriptions. Moreover, all those brave programs of linguistic reform, undertaken in the hope of framing a language more adequate to the representation of the world, are generated from the same assumption and are equally fallacious. It is like demanding that the word for wood be itself wooden ("ink" then being one of the few philosophically satisfactory words in written English). It goes without saying that language plays sly tricks, and especially upon philosophers whose medium is language: so a measure of regimentation is only sanitary. But the programs I have in mind go beyond prophylaxis: their criterion of adequacy is parity of structure with the world, taken as the mirror-image of an ideal language and, hence, linguistic itself. But the conditions for adequate description surely do not compass parity of form, and once we renounce formal parities, the imputation of ineffability on the world's part and inadequacy on language's part becomes logically unstrung. My view is that the whole of philosophy may be appreciated as a response to this merely bogus semantical theory, that the history of metaphysics from Plato to Wittgenstein consists of so many mythic embroideries upon it. But that is a thesis for another book.

The "rectification of names" was a constant preoccupation of the classical Chinese philosophers, it being their view that misperception, especially in moral matters, rested upon misdescription. Their aims, as those of their peers in India, were never merely philosophical, but always practical and often urgent. Yet there is more than this to the demotion of discourse in Lao Tzu's poem. There is, in addition, a systematic deflation of that sort of knowledge exemplified in knowing that a certain proposition is true: what we may term propositional knowledge. Such knowledge has been, certainly in the intellectualist traditions of the West, largely favored as the fulfillment of our cognitive ambitions; and when there has been one or another of those skeptical despairs of the kind epistemologists make a profession of discovering and surmounting, they have been seen as threats to that certitude in which the mind finds repose. Post-Cartesian philosophy has often been an exercise in logical vigilance against doubts of a sort that bear only upon propositional knowledge. But the knowledge Lao Tzu celebrates is of quite another order, and is immune to these. We may understand it, I believe, by thinking for a moment of the image of the Way, the *Tao*, upon which Lao Tzu elaborates a series of stunning poetic appreciations.

A way is something we follow. It is something that can be stumbled across or pointed out: it can be lost and found again: it can be discovered. To know the way is to be able to arrive at a destination without getting lost. So knowledge of the way is a matter of performance and execution: of *doing* something rather than *believing* something that is true: it is knowing *how*, in Gilbert Ryle's influential (and unwittingly Taoist) disjunction, in contrast with knowing *that* (something is the case). Since it is practical rather than propositional, and because it implies action rather than description, it connects with the counterverbal theme of the poem, which has the paradoxical status of any words whose intent is to undo words as a class. But on the other hand, the way the founders of Taoism employ words is not altogether discursive. The *Tao Te Ching*, as pointed out already, is a prose poem, and Chuang Tzu, perhaps the most delightful writer in any literature, employed parables in his work. Here is one, translated by Arthur Waley, which bears upon the immediate topic. It concerns a wheelwright, who tells the Duke of Ch'i that the book he is reading, since by dead men, is only "lees and scum."

> *Speaking as a wheelwright . . . I look at the matter in this way; when I am making a wheel, if my stroke is too slow, then it bites deep but is not steady; if my stroke is too fast, then it is steady but does not go deep. The right pace, neither slow nor fast, cannot get into the hand unless it comes from the heart. It is a thing that cannot be put into words; there is an art in it that I cannot explain to my son. That is why it is impossible for me to let him take over my work, and here I am, at the age of seventy, still making wheels. In my opinion it must have been the same with the men of old. All that was worth handing on, died with them; the rest they put in books. That is why I said that what you were reading was the lees and scum of bygone men.*

What the wheelwright says in unexceptionable, and would be correct if what men sought to put in books were what cannot be put there: and even then it is not plain that were he as clever with words as with spokeshaves, he would be still unable to transfer practical knowledge from fingers to page. There is in any case no possible way of assimilating discursive to practical knowledge or conversely, though philosophers, in their characteristic mania for monisms, have tried to achieve such reductions. To know how is to engage causally with the world, and by following the way, the practical knower contributes to the shape the world takes: converting sticks into spokes, to take the characteristically homely example. By contrast, knowing that something is the case is to stand, as it were, outside the world, which then is set over and against the proposition it makes true. Language has a performative and a descriptive aspect: as performative, it is employed as a force, if only in society, in modulating the shape of things. As descriptive, by contrast, it stands to reality in the kind of relationship a chart does. We may steer by charts, but we will succeed in arriving, save by lucky accident, only to the degree that the chart is accurate: and it is the relationships, through which we may speak of accuracy and truth, in virtue of which language may be considered external to the reality it represents. Knowledge as performance and representation is irreducibly duplex, and Lao Tzu is essentially correct when he implies that words, used at least descriptively, are logically external to the reality they record, and that there is a dimension of existence that could not possibly be put in words. The rest of his teaching is a deprecation of one sort of knowledge in favor of another.

There is another contrast. It is difficult to see what sense might attach to the claim that I know it to be raining out, but *do not know it very well.* Propositional knowledge has no place for degrees and comparisons. Practical knowledge does: I may say I know how to ride a horse, but I do not know how to ride as well as Jane. I struggle where she does not. Practical knowledge enables some to be better than others, but strugglers do not know the Way. The Way is smooth to those who know it. This sort of smoothness is prized by Taoists. The feeling of effort is the inner translation of ignorance of the way: hence effortlessness is the sign of knowledge. The Principle of Least Effort, as we shall see, formulates the situation of maximal competence.

The Way is a marvelous allusive image, and includes in its connotative array the suggestive metaphor of the road or path. Taoist literature and art is full of wanderers: but the road they are on leads nowhere particularly. It is not *la dirrita via* that Dante lost in middle life and found again. It is simply a thread through space. Taoist landscapes are clouds and mists, which part to reveal the fragment of a road. A path winds across a scroll simply to disappear in some grey wash. The paradigm Taoist figure is a wanderer: "Days and months are travellers of

eternity," wrote the poet Bashō, the great Japanese master of
the *haiku* form:

> *So are the years that pass by. Those who steer a boat across*
> *the sea or drive a horse over the earth till they succumb to*
> *the weight of years, spend every minute of their lives trav-*
> *elling. There are a number of ancients, too, who died on the*
> *road. I myself have been tempted for a long time by the*
> *cloud-moving wind—filled with a strong desire to wander.*

"Determined to fall / A weather-exposed skeleton," he writes in
one of his travel books, Bashō is not a man with a destination.
He is no Dante, puffing up an arduous path through a hierar-
chical universe to a permanent lodging in Paradise. The Way
has no vector. One cannot get lost. The Way is everywhere.
With Dante, and the road he emblemized, the price of being
lost is momentous, and men need a guide if not a savior to find
their way. Nor is knowing the way something a man can get
good at or improve himself in, for there is no time for practice.
Moreover, there is only one way. Lao Tzu's way is not of this
sort. The price one pays for not finding it is manageable, since
it is simply frustration and unhappiness, not eternal damnation.
And any way will serve. The *Tao* is merely the grain of the
world, and Lao Tzu is urging only a natural life in the sense
that we should not live against the grain. So the wanderer does
not follow an itinerary, like a pilgrim thirsting for the final
beatitudes. Happiness is the way one goes, not something lumi-
nous at the end. Of course, there is no rest there: we are always moving, as in the *Gita* we are always acting. But we can
move without effort, and that is what following the Way is.

There is something in Dante that is strenuous: the way is
hard and upward, and it demands a struggle that would be a
sign for Lao Tzu that we were lost after all. Following the
path involves, for him, submission. When we are not enjoined
to regard the infant as the paradigm of how we should be in
the world, we are told to be as women, to conquer through ·

yielding, to find the path through letting the path find us. By this, I believe, Lao Tzu is saying that we ought not try to impose our will upon a world to which it is alien. Imposing will and order almost seems to be a formula for going against the grain, and hence for frustration, disharmony, and unhappiness. And, once again, the absence of struggle emerges as the sign of being rightly in the world. Chuang Tzu provides a wonderfully concrete example of this in another Taoist personage, this time the butcher Ting:

> When this carver Ting was carving a bull for the king, every touch of his hand, every inclination of the shoulder, every step he trod, every pressure of the knee, while swiftly and lightly he wielded his carving knife, was as carefully timed as the movement of a dancer. . . . "Wonderful," said the king. "I could never have believed that the art of carving could reach such a point as this." "I am a lover of Tao," replied Ting, putting away his knife, "and have succeeded in applying it to the art of carving."

Ting claims to have gazed at the animals he worked upon until he saw the body as a set of natural parts. He apprehended it then with his soul rather than his eyes, and his knife found the natural lines of cleavage—"and so by conforming my work to the structure with which I am dealing, I have reached a point at which my knife never touches even the smallest ligament or tendon, let alone the main gristle."

> Where part meets part, there is always space. And a knife blade has no thickness. Insert an instrument which has no thickness into a structure that is amply spaced, and surely it cannot fail to have plenty of room. That is why I can use a blade for nineteen years, and yet it still looks as though it were fresh from the forger's mould.

The *Tao Te Ching* often speaks of the utility of emptiness, and the image of everything being achieved when nothing is penetrated by nothing justifies the king's satisfaction with Ting's observation: "This interview with the carver Ting has taught me how man's vital forces can be conserved."

Ting contrasts his way of working with that of the ordinary hacker "continually twisting and turning [his knife] like a worm burrowing through the earth." In effect, the bull—and by implication anything—sunders into its natural fragments when one learns its Way and hence learns not to work. Efficiency is increased as effort is decreased, as though the former approaches infinity as the latter approaches zero, and in the ideal case, which is obviously the impossible promise of Taoism, one should be able by doing nothing to achieve everything. Indeed, almost exactly this principle, albeit hardly expressed in the mocking idiom of the calculus I have employed, is embodied in the concept of *Wu Wei*, "do nothing," which is what I want especially to stress in this chapter because of its moral implications. *Wu Wei*, nondoing, celebrates the power of immobility.

It is somewhat ironic that the most explicit discussions of *Wu Wei*—Taoist exposition is, suitable perhaps to the subject it discusses, veiled in mists and conceptual cloudiness—are to be found in a body of singularly Machiavellian writings on politics, those of the Legalists. These comprise, as their analogue in the West, advice to a prince. The structure of government is to be so arranged that the prince may have maximal power with minimal or no effort, the latter being virtually a condition for the former. As it happens, this requires a political structure of the most crushing repressiveness, in which each individual is bound by terror to function at a level of total competence. The slightest deviation or infraction will be massively punished by functionaries who are themselves under the threat of massive punishment for derelictions interpreted in the strictest terms. The entire edifice of counterposed terror and strict severity in the determination of duty operates mechanically, like a solar system, in the center of which the emperor

sits like the sun, the one immobile entity in the whole structure. Each part is held in prescribed orbit by others held in
theirs, the entirety to last forever. This system was tried, as a
matter of fact, and of course it failed, but the conception itself
reveals a dominating fear of instability and anarchy, social dis-
organization and political chaos, to which Confucianism,
Taoism, and Legalism were meant to respond and to rem-
edy. Strife and unpredictability were symptoms of not having
found the way, and fear of these expressed itself in a kind of
natural conservatism which is present even in Maoist thought
and the Cultural Revolution in China. For is not that, too, an
attempt so to modify the human material of the state as to
forestall any possibility of change from without? And to build
something ultimately immune to disintegration through internal conflict?

Wu Wei promises, as this sort of thought usually does, a
great deal for a very little. So, for that matter does Taoism,
and indeed its commercial underside must have swamped the
original teaching, much as though, to take a Western example,
one were to pursue meekness as a means for inheriting the
earth, which is a considerable bargain. This kind of promise
blemishes Taoism's original edifying teaching, but it is a common enough, human-all-too-human phenomenon, as we have
seen. Yoga, which is a fairly austere doctrine, nevertheless,
promises great and practical powers, advertised even in the
Yoga Sutra virtually as inducements for embarking upon a
mode of spiritual exercises whose inherent value is publicized
as transcendent. It is like promising a state of utter bliss and
then suggesting reasons for pursuing it: like amplified sexual
power, the ability to dominate and influence people, or to win
at the stock market. Taoism as a movement hardened into a religion with saints and rituals, and petered out in the usual superstition and rigamarole, the search for the Way degenerating
into the quest for elixirs of immortality and the like. In popular fiction Lao Tzu himself is depicted as a kind of mad

alchemical scientist. But this is only the vulgar nether side, the translation into crass vehicles, to which any idea of whatever degree of sublimity is liable in the traffic of acceptance. Let us rather think of it in its better light. The idea that *Wu Wei* exemplifies is rather like the idea of the Discipline of Action in the *Gita*, without its karmic considerations, which must be classed as inducements in their own right, and so at odds with the anticonsequentialist posture the Discipline of Action imposes. Let us think of these ideas without reference to profit. The sage Mencius visited King Hui of Liang. "You have not considered a thousand *li* too far to come, and must therefore have something of profit to offer my kingdom," the king said. "Let your majesty speak only of humanity and righteousness," Mencius replied. "Why must you speak of *profit?*" Let us discuss matters, then, in Mencius' terms.

The *Tao Te Ching* has a natural appeal to artists. It describes to perfection certain high moments of artistic work, those moments of pure creativity, when artist and work are not separated by a gap of any sort, but fuse in such a way that the work seems to bring itself into existence. At such points —and any creative person lives for these—there is none of the struggle and externality that mark those phases of artistic labor in which inspiration fails and the work itself refuses to cooperate. Of course, art is not the only activity in which there is this mutual yielding. Levin's sublimation to the activity of mowing, in *Anna Karenina*, is as exalting and very much in the Taoist spirit, which, with its weavers and butchers and wheelwrights, is refreshingly unimpressed with Art as some particularly privileged activity. What Levin loses is a sense of apartness from the processes he is engaged in, becoming, for a blissful interval, one with those processes. Struggle and effort are here the marks of apartness, and what the *Tao Te Ching* is urging, finally, is this loss of self. If there is an injunction, it is to find the way the world wants to go and then to take that way oneself: and not to attempt to impose one's own order onto things, not to dominate. Or to achieve domination by surrendering up the will. The famous illustration of this is in the art of archery, where one must let the arrow find its way to the target, the highest art being the absolute absence of art. Arrows, brushes, scythes, and spokeshaves are instruments of release, not means to profit, and ultimately they are agents of selflessness, which is the state at which, along with so much of Oriental philosophy, Taoism aims.

Of course, these attitudes towards skill must reinforce the anti-intellectual tendency that is never far beneath the surface, that distrust of artfulness in favor of simplicity that Tolstoy predictably adopted as an aesthetic and moral stance. Hence it naturally goes with an elevation of the lowly, already seen in Lao Tzu's celebration of infants, children, and artisans, and which, with the curious exception of Hinduism, seems to be a propensity of religions: perhaps because religion must emphasize the final helplessness of men in order to render urgent the promise and fortunate availability of help from without. Christ propounded many paradoxes in delivering his doctrine, but none perhaps more dissonant with Roman common sense than the claim that the poor and miscast are actually superior persons. Charity was a widely enough practiced virtue in the Mediterranean world, and large-handedness has always been felt as an obligation of the high, if only as an emblem of their highness: one could even have understood an argument that men have certain duties toward the unfortunate in life. But to insist that the unfortunate are actually better, that one can do nothing better than to emulate the low: this must have sounded as incoherent as the darkest stanzas of the mystics. Surely the sentimentalizing of the proletariat on the part of Marxists is only a transformation of Christ's curious transvaluation, just as Mao's injunction to go to the peasants is not merely a revolutionary strategy. It is only the latest form of an attitude deep in the traditions of the *Tao*.

It was only natural that Lao Tzu should extend the principle of nonintervention to the art of government, the acquisition of which was the dominating preoccupation of the classical philosophers of China. He rather perplexingly recommended that one should govern a province the way one fries small fish, which commentators suppose must mean that one does not intervene in the lives of the governed: small fish disintegrate into a mess with too much stirring. So the best government is the least government, a thesis the Legalists would have endorsed in the abstract, since it is exactly the doctrine of *Wu Wei*, though Lao Tzu intended, one feels, merely a genial anarchism. In addition to the wanderer and the artisan, the personae of Taoist literature rounds out with the eccentric and the oddball, the man incapable of being governed, who does not fit in, like a twisted peg. As with so much of Taoism, the thought that political felicity consists in permitting things to find their natural course is optimistic and radically naive: "If the *Tao* prevailed in the world," Confucius wryly observed, "I should not be trying to alter things." The fact that he was trying was in Taoist eyes a sign that he had not found the way, but the perversion of this form of thought is to make the culmination of skill the point at which one must begin: as though no effort were required in order to achieve the treasured state of effortlessness.

The celebration of quirkiness; the image of the hermit on the mountain slope; the cheery tramp pausing en route to nowhere to admire the scene; the potter, the archer, the drunk poet: these take on a certain poignancy in the Chinese context, which was after all defined by the triumph of Confucian ethics. The Confucian is concerned with duty, family, role, and obligation, and in principle desires only to be of use. Locked into a rigid system of deferences and rituals, the maintenance of which he saw as a charm against chaos whatever its intrinsic value, the Confucian must have seen in Taoism a dazzling freedom and escape. There is a very moving fragment in the *Analects* to this effect. Confucius was speaking with his followers. The constant topic of the conversation is what they would do were they given the opportunity to govern. In fact, of course, they were largely excluded, and their discussions are thus as speculative as those of emigrés from a successful revolution. In this passage, one after another describes what he would do were his wishes granted: good, useful things. The last to speak is Tseng Hsi. "I am afraid," he says, "That my wishes are entirely different from those cherished by these gentlemen."

> *In the latter days of spring, when the light spring garments are made, I would like to take along five or six grown-ups and six or seven youths to bathe in the river Yi, and after the bath go to enjoy the breeze in the woods among the altars of Wu-yi and then return home, loitering and singing on our way.*

Confucius is described as heaving a deep sigh. "You are the man after my own heart," he said.

It is the tension between and ultimately the harmonization of Confucian and Taoist traits that formed the typical character of the Chinese mind. It is the Taoist spirit we admire in those pale grey landscapes of the Sung dynasty, where the individual barely punctuates the formless mists in which mountains are washed in as vague, dreamful forms. But these paintings were done by Confucianists, men who had gone through the taxing system of state examinations to become civil servants. The paintings thus testify, almost painfully, to the constricting meshwork of relationships state and family caught a man up in. They are fantasies of freedom. In one of the *Analects* Confucius passes two Taoists. They are farming. "The whole world is swept as by a torrential flood," they say, "And who can change it?" One should flee the world! Confucius ruefully observes that "One cannot herd together with birds and beasts. If I am not to be a man among other men, then what am I to be?" And it is here he makes the point that one has to work to change things, that one cannot simply conform to the drift. So, though his heart may indeed be with Tseng Hsi, he has no real alternative as a man. The question is not whether to impose an order, but which order to impose. And this was the burden of his thought.

With Confucius one begins to get a glimpse of something that has been lacking in the philosophies we have touched upon in this book, namely a genuine moral idea. Taoism pictures the person as a wanderer in the void, and perceives his happiness to lie in drifting with the stream, unanchored by the network of demands and responsibilities. The Confucian, by contrast, has endorsed and internalized these responsibilities and yields to them, sacrificing or postponing his own happiness if need be, or merely identifying it with moral submission. In this, I believe, Taoism is the more typically Oriental attitude. The happiness one is concerned with is one's own, logically independent of the happiness of others. Only in the teaching of Mahayana do we, perhaps, get a different idea, but even there, the happiness in question is the absolute bliss of Nirvana, as though nothing less than that had any bearing on human concern. Morality is bound up with the felicities and distractions of common life, and its satisfactions are so minor compared with salvation as to stand in no possible proportion to the latter: and salvation then is irrelevant to its satisfaction. Happiness, of course, is what men always want, not, as Aristotle pointed out, as a means to anything but always as an end: "in order to . . ." is never an appropriate answer to the question, if it has an appropriate answer, of why we want to be happy. And cynics are inclined to suggest that we, in fact, never do act for any reason, however we may represent the matter to ourselves, save one, which bears upon the promotion of our own happiness. So, cynics might argue, even if one postpones his own happiness in order to do his duty, is it not plain that he finds a greater happiness in doing his duty than not, and hence acts as selfishly as one who sees no point in de-

ferring his, and who is honestly egotistic, as we all are *au fond*
though perhaps less honestly? Well, this may be a compelling
thought, but one has blurred a crucial distinction in treating
happiness as though it did not have a moral category. The
pursuit of happiness takes on a moral quality when one's own
happiness becomes contingent upon the happiness of others, or
at least what one believes is the happiness of others. No man
could be counted moral who did not have that minimal concern for others that permits his own felicitude to vary as theirs
does. This, surely, is what Confucius implies when he speaks
of being a man among men. He does not imply merely to be
one among many, a person in a crowd, not even a member of
society in which one derives comfort and convenience from the
labors of others (and they of your labors), so that one's welfare
is a function of the system as a whole: like an organ in an organic system. This is to see others, in Kant's phrase, as means,
even if one sees oneself as a means as well and realizes that one
cannot get what one wants without functioning usefully
within the system. None of these ways of being among men
has any special moral color.

Confucius is sometimes credited with having formed a ver-
sion of the Golden Rule with his principle of reciprocity.
"What I do not wish others to do unto me, I also wish not to
do unto others." This is voiced by one of the disciples, Tuan-
mu Tz'u, and Confucius sharply says: "You are not up to
that," implying that it is not easy to apply: Tuan-mu is only
repeating a lesson. It is a lesson we will be impressed with
more or less depending upon how impressed we are with the
Golden Rule itself, which any freshmen in philosophy can gun
down with two or three sharp questions, for all the moral
guidance it can give. But the major insight of the great teaching remains, namely that how others feel about our actions towards them should be internally related to our feelings about
those actions, and hence their feelings should penetrate our
motives. And this is the force of "among" in being a man

among men. If our own happiness rises and falls in causal consequence of our beliefs about the happiness of others (and a man is genuinely evil who can be happy only when and because others are unhappy), it may be that the aggregate happiness would be less than were each of us to pursue his own felicity oblivious to the feelings of others. One cannot but consider that possibility when one reckons the principle of greatest aggregate happiness, which has been advanced by Utilitarians, for it is possible that the moral state of affairs comes out to a lower quantity, in which case some criterion other than the greatest aggregate happiness is required for morality, and Utilitarianism can hardly furnish that. In any case, considerateness is the foundation of a moral attitude, and while it is inhumane to restrict this only to other humans— one may after all consider the undeniable feelings of animals and within limits count on them considering ours—one cannot be "among" birds and beasts since the limits of moral education there are narrow at best. Moral education, to which Confucius devoted immense attention, consists less in the inculcation of rules, which is only moral training and can be given to dogs, but in getting men to assume attitudes towards themselves that are logically connected with the attitudes others take towards themselves. When my actions towards x are illuminated by the reading x will assign them, x and I form a nuclear moral community, and assuming that the psychological conditions for reciprocity requires me to see x, and indeed all members of it, as individuals conscious of themselves as selves and of others as the same: a "kingdom of ends," in Kant's rather heavy phrase. But none of this, for all its emphasis upon eccentricity and skewed behavior, is the main teaching of Taoism. Neither, for the matter, is Taoism impressed with that condition which is the mirror image of morality, its "pathological" counterpart, regarded I believe mistakenly by some as the basis of morality: namely love. Love dawns when the happiness of another person takes one's own happiness in hostage, and in consequence is something the cynical may regard as bondage and which has its sad or comical possibilities, especially when the happiness of the other is indifferent to the one who has tied his happiness to it. Liberation from affect, which is the aim and therapy of Taoism, clearly cannot compass love nor even its analogy in moral concern. The follower of the Way is necessarily a loner, though hardly lonely, which is part of its undeniable appeal.

Let me put the contrast in a somewhat different light. The classical philosophers of China were moralists and philosophical anthropologists rather than, as a general rule, epistemologists or metaphysicians. One great question defined and divided the structure of debate among them, namely that of the original nature of man. Confucius claimed that we are close by nature and far apart only through our practices. So changes in practice might bring us to a closer acknowledgement that all are brothers. At least difference in behavior does not mean a difference in essence: we owe a certain dignity to all men, however curious we find their behavior: and we can blame the institutions under which they grew up for any derelictions we may find. Mencius goes so far as to say men are by nature good: no man is so far gone, he argues, that he would not reflexively try to save a baby about to fall down a well. Hence the way to universal welfare is through revisions in practices. The terms, then, in which the 'original nature' of man was debated were moral ones, and as there is a law of philosophical controversy that requires all positions to be occupied, we find alongside Mencius' the theses that man is by nature evil; that he is neither good nor evil; and that he is both good and evil. The matrix of discussion was fixed for ages, much in the same way that the wrangle over human freedom was set in the West. As always, the issue had to seem practical, since the shape of institutions differ depending upon whether we have to liberate a native goodness or confine a native wickedness. Taoism is a radical teaching in that it takes its stands outside all the available positions, rejecting them as a class. It comes into the plane of discussion at right angles, so to speak, with a kind of religious impetus.

I once heard the Ninth Symphony of Beethoven performed under the coffered vaults of the Basilica of Constantine in the Forum in Rome. It is a powerful and stirring work, but even so, the setting was disproportionate to the content, and when a huge chorus sang the "All men will be brothers," those sentiments were diminished to pointlessness by the dumb masses of the ruin above them, arching like a Marabar Cave. In something like this disproportion, Taoism seems to dissolve any relations we may have to one another and to replace them with the relationship we have to the universe at large. The question it poses is the question we appear to encounter broadcast through the Orient, namely how to close the gap between the world and ourselves, how to "lose" the self. Whereas it is just that gap that is presupposed by the moral questions of classical China and perhaps by the concept of morality itself. They suppose the gaps that need closing are those that separate us from one another. However, these are not relevant in closing the gap between the Way and ourselves, which is the source of the only kind of infelicitude thinkers like Lao Tzu regard as worth healing and, perhaps, the only kind they are capable of healing. So these are lines of thought that can at best intersect, since they lie in different planes and cannot really conflict. Or, if you wish, the conflicts between the Confucians and the other classical philosophers are of a different order than that between them and Lao Tzu. Or better: however they may be divided among themselves, they are each divided in the same way against Lao Tzu. That opposition makes metaphysical brothers of them all, and their discord merely sibling.

Taoism, like the Karma-Yoga of the *Gita*, is a teaching that aims at the stunning of the will, and I believe that generally the mechanism of the will is considered the enemy of ultimate happiness throughout the East. "It might be better to flow

away monotonously, like the river," one of Charles Dickens'
characters muses, "and to compound for its insensibility to
happiness with its insensibility to pain." The sages would con-
cur with this, except with regard to happiness, perhaps: they
would urge that the happinesses Clenham has in mind are inextricably bound up with pains, and that there is an even and
unbroken happiness of another order to be found by just this
monotonous flowing away, of being at one with the stream.
But then it is extremely difficult to derive a moral philosophy
on the basis of this if the very possibility of morality presupposes the mechanism of the will and the possibility of acting
contrary to or deliberately in what one takes to be conformity
with the world. Exactly that space that Taoism intends to collapse is what makes morality possible at all.

By this, I mean the possibility of morality as such, not this
or that moral system. That morality is not natural could be
argued on the basis of the plurality of moral systems that pre-
vail, unless one supposes that those who practice them belong
to different species. It is consistent with the concept of morality, then, that there should be different moral structures.
The only moral universals, if there are any, would be those
that follow from the concept of morality as such, and so must
be part of every moral system. It would be a great philosophical achievement to deduce specific moral principles from the
principle of morality itself, comparable to that hoped for by
St. Anselm, when he believed he had discovered a concept that
entailed its own nonemptiness. Accordingly, this concept
could not be understood without knowing that it had an instance, so we, in fact, know it to have an instance because we
understand it. I regard Anselm's enterprise as illegitimate, but
not so its counterpart in moral philosophy. I shall not attempt
to undertake this deduction in the present work, nor even de-
fend it. It does, however, entail a kind of censure of the philosophies of Lao Tzu and the others we have discussed, Confucius being an exception, because in enjoining the collapse of

the conditions that made morality possible, they fall under a moral violation by our criterion. And so they merit blame of a kind. We might hardly find moral guidance there, then, and perhaps not in religion at all, so far as these schools of thought are paradigms of religious thinking.

SUGGESTED READINGS

Those readers motivated to further explorations in Oriental literatures will find remarkably useful as a first baedeker W. T. de Bary and A. Embree (eds.) *A Guide to Oriental Classics* (New York: Columbia University Press, 1964). In addition to a canon of great works of Islam, China, India, and Japan, the *Guide* lists and comments upon the adequacy of various translations, and provides bibliographies of the more accessible secondary works. Good bibliographies may be found appended to the appropriate articles in Paul Edwards (ed.), *The Encyclopedia of Philosophy* (New York: Macmillan and Free Press, 1967), the articles themselves being sound surveys of Oriental philosophy. For magisterial but largely expository histories of Indian and Chinese philosophy respectively, consult Surendranath Dasgupta, *A History of Indian Philosophy*, 5 vols. (New York: Cambridge University Press, 1922–1955); and Fung Yu-Lan, *History of Chinese Philosophy*, Dirk Bodde (trans.), 2 vols (Princeton, New Jersey: Princeton University Press, 1952–1953). A brighter, shorter book by far is H. G. Creel's *Chinese Thought from Confucius to Mao Tze Tung* (New York: New American Library, Mentor, 1953). Nothing comparable to Creel is available for India. Heinrich Zimmer, *Philosophies of India* (New York: Meridian, 1956), is suggestive and original but unlimpid, while Chandradhar Sharma, *Indian Philosophy: A Critical Survey* (New York: Barnes & Noble, 1962) is dry and orthodox. Karl Potter, *Presuppositions of India's Philosophies* (Englewood Cliffs: Prentice-Hall, 1964) is synoptic, but philosophers are more likely to derive benefits from Ninian Smart, *Doctrine and Argument in Indian Philosophy* (London: Allen and Unwin, 1964), which is analytical in orientation while sympathetic in attitude. Krishnachandra Bhattacharya, *Philosophical Studies* (Calcutta: Progressive Publishers, 1958), Volume 1, has interpretive essays by a major thinker on the classical philosophies: Volume 2 contains Bhattacharya's own statement, which is a major contribution by a philosopher of world importance, though largely neglected in the West. I. C. Sharma, *Ethical Philosophies of India* (Lincoln, Nebraska: Johnsen Publishing Co., 1965) delivers what the title promises, but once more in orthodox perspective. It is worth reading, however, for the perspective itself. Returning to China, Arthur Waley, *Three Ways of Thought in Ancient China* (New York: Anchor Books, 1959) is an absolute delight, which weaves translation and comment into a manageable picture of Taoism, Confucianism, and Legalism. Joseph Needham puts Chinese philosophy in an original light as Volume 2 of his monumental *Science and Civilization in China* (New York: Cambridge University Press, 1956).

The volumes compiled under the direction of de Bary for the Oriental Civilization courses at Columbia—*Sources of the Indian Tradition* (New York: Columbia University Press, 1958) and *Sources of Chinese Tradition* (New York: Columbia University Press, 1961)—present substantial selections from philosophical and religious writings and put them in their contexts in illuminatings ways. There is also a volume on Japan. I have found Max Weber, *The Religion of China* (New York: Free Press, 1951) and *The Religion of India* (New York: Free Press, 1958) exceedingly helpful in seeing Oriental religions against their institutional bases.

I add now some translations of major works, of use to those not near libraries apt to stock Orientalia. The following brief roster includes what I regard as fine translations which are also in paperback format. I cite the paperback edition in each case, rather than the original publisher.

The Analects of Confucius, trans. Arthur Waley (New York: Modern Library, 1938).

The Bhagavad Gita, tr. Franlin Edgerton (New York: Harper Torchbooks, 1964).

Burtt, E. A., *The Teachings of the Compassionate Buddha* (New York: New American Library, 1955).

Mencius, trans. D. C. Lau (London: Penguin, 1970).

The Questions of King Milinda (Milindapanha), trans. T. W. Rhys-Davids (New York: Dover, 1963), 2 vols.

The Thirteen Principle Upanishads, trans. Robert Hume (Oxford: Oxford University Press, 1971).

The Vedanta Sutras of Badarayana, with Commentary by Sankara, trans. George Thibault (New York: Dover, 1962), 2 vols.

The Way and its Power, trans. Arthur Waley (New York: Evergreen, 1958).

INDEX